911 FROM AN INSIDE LINE

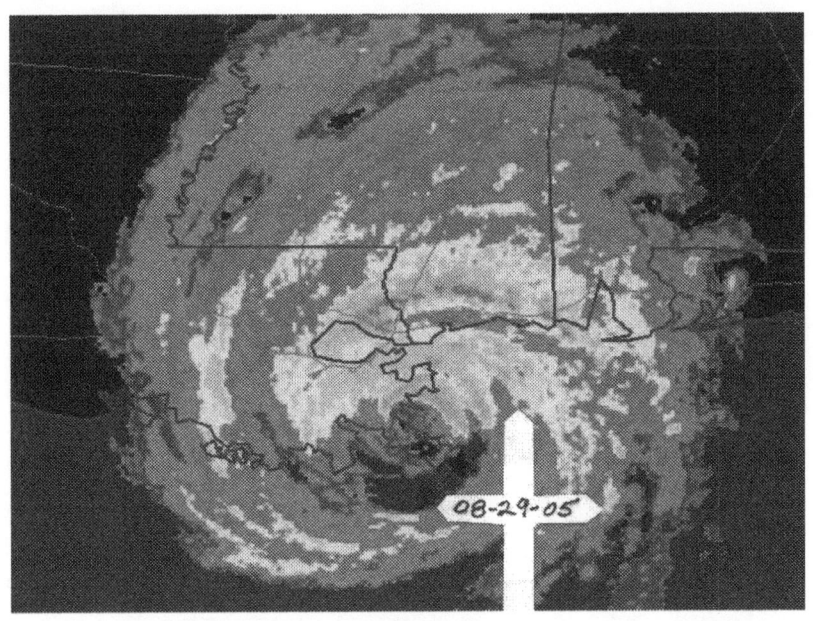

911 FROM AN
INSIDE LINE

A WAVELAND, MS POLICE DISPATCHER'S ACCOUNT OF HURRICANE
KATRINA AND MIRACLES AND TRUTHS FROM THE GULF COAST

DENISE STEPHENSON

To order additional copies of this book, contact:
Xlibris Corporation
1-888-795-4274
www.Xlibris.com
Orders@Xlibris.com

38682

CONTENTS

Chapter 1

Chapter 2

Chapter 3

Chapter 4

"It's only when you lose everything that you are truly free to do anything"

Unknown Author

These words were displayed on the sign out in front of Our Lady of the Gulf Catholic Church located on Beach Boulevard in Bay St. Louis, MS for at least a week before Hurricane Katrina hit the area. I wondered at the time how these words related to my own life. After the disaster I realized that they were prophetic. I have repeated these words in my mind many, many times since August 29, 2005 and have found comfort and hope and courage in them.

Authors Note

This book is in honor of my Mother . . . . Her faith, her courage through even the roughest times, and her contagious optimism has always encouraged me to "just keep going and things will get better". I have written this book to share these events and my personal truths with my children, my future grandchildren and their children yet to come. I want them to know that nothing in this world is impossible to overcome when we stay sure of who we are and always keep our eyes on Jesus. I am living proof of that.

God has given me a story that aches to be told. It is about Mother Nature, the instinct to survive and miracles that still happen even today. It is about nurturing our children (train up a child in the way he should go . . . . Proverbs 22:6) and keeping faith in all circumstances. It is about the real truth of no man being an island, and about the true meaning of love one another. It will frighten you, enlighten you and possibly even bring a tear or two. My hope is that it will inspire you to strengthen your faith . . . . believing without seeing.

This is a recount from inside the eye wall of the Beast—Hurricane Katrina, as it came ashore in Waveland, MS. This is just as I experienced it and lived to tell about it. I was there, working alongside all of the other Waveland Police Department employees, and this is how I remember that morning—August 29, 2005. We struggled as individuals and stuck together as a team, and we all survived.

The truths as I have expressed them here are my personal experiences that I have encountered along the road to recovery from the worst natural disaster that our United States has ever known.

CHAPTER 1

THE WEEKEND BEFORE ~ ~ AUGUST 26-28, 2005

It was two days before she made landfall when we were put on "stand by" in preparation of her coming. Little did any of us know just how unprepared we would be for her visit. We had been through this preparation phase many, many times before and had always weathered whatever Mother Nature handed us. Living on the Gulf Coast had its benefits in spite of the occasional inconveniences that the threat of bad weather brought. We had seen so many come and go, teasing us as they skirted our coastline and then sparing us the final blow. Maybe it was complacency, but we prepared all the same as we always had before, only sharing our fears quietly with each other. Our conversations were shared in a joking way and with a certain amount of excitement in our voices as we anticipated what was to come over these next few days. None of us could have imagined, not even in our wildest dreams, the events that were about to unfold in front of us. It would prove to be the single most life changing event any of us had ever faced.

My weekend off had just begun and I was more than ready for some relaxation and fun. After working 12 hour night shifts in a dispatch office, I was looking forward to a night out on the town. It was early afternoon and I had already started thinking about how I would spend that evening. I knew my weekend might possibly be cut short due to some storm way down in the Southeast part of the Gulf . . . . her name was Katrina and no one was quite sure yet which path she would decide to take. Not to worry though, we had NOAA watching her and I had a night off work!

Bay Saint Louis, MS was truly a place set apart from the rest of the world. Its natural beauty and its Southern laid-back lifestyle made it a priceless gem for all of us lucky enough to have lived there. Many people drifted through there but it seemed only a selected few decided to stay and call it home on a full time basis. I had been fortunate enough to have lived there for only a little over four years, but it had honestly felt like home to me from day one. I lived in an old wood framed house just a block and a half off the beach, and I could sit on my back screened in porch and hear the waves rolling in and out and smell that wonderful salt water on the breeze. It was heaven to me . . . . truly a place of peace and calmness. I had left the hectic life of Memphis, TN and a twenty-five year marriage to get there, but it was worth the life change for me.

Most of the people living there on the coast of that bay were creative and free-spirited, and their artwork of all sorts imaginable could be seen throughout the entire town. From painted murals to great music, along with superb food and festivals for every reason or just for no reason at all, life there was special. The fishermen sold their daily catch right from the boats each day, and the talented chefs cooked it all up and we all ate well every day. My house was just seven blocks from the notorious "Old Town", and I could always smell the scents from the cooking wafting my way from all the restaurants down on the beachfront. Fresh shrimp and oysters were always a delight, but even the steaks and hot dogs tasted better there for some unknown reason. Many a meal was celebrated with a shave ice and a leisurely stroll along Beach Boulevard as the perfect "dessert". I've often wondered how many dreams were manifested as people walked along there, gazing in awe at the wonder of that beautiful Gulf and seeing the magic of where the ocean meets the sky. For me, I always felt that there were no limits to the possibilities in life when I stood there and gazed at all that beauty . . . . it always, always set my spirit free and allowed it to soar high above the ocean and the sky. I suspect it did that for most of us living there. Having been born on Galveston Island, TX and raised very near there, I have often said that I have salt water running through my veins. I know for a fact that you cannot take a fish out of water and expect it to survive. My life was simply better by the sea, and I can only guess how long it will be before I will return there. Sometimes I can still hear the waves and taste the salt on my skin, and if it's a very, very good day, I can feel the spray lightly kissing my face and washing all my cares away. My life was simply better by the sea, and I pray that God will bless me with a little spot in heaven just like Bay Saint Louis, MS when I get to the other side. I've been so lucky to have seen it and experienced it first hand, and I will surely hope that heaven will be just like that when I get there.

Getting back to that weekend, I have to tell you that not one person who remained on that coast ever thought she would strike with such force and destroy as much as she did. Not even in yours or our imaginations, could we have ever dreamed it. Certainly those of us who stayed never envisioned the death and destruction she would leave behind. I stayed only because it was a requirement of my job, and it was made very clear that if I chose to leave, I would have no job when I returned. As silly as that may sound now, it was a very real threat to me at the time and I would not risk losing my job. Had I known, if only I had known. It's all for naught now, and job requirements for me have now become self imposed, rather than being dictated to me by someone else. Had I listened to my instincts, which I choose to believe is Divine intervention in my life, I most certainly would have been long gone from there without question or hesitation. Nonetheless, I stayed. I did have some divine intervention that weekend though in that my daughter, who was living with me, left against her will and judgment only about 12 hours before Katrina made landfall. We have yet to find a trace of her bedroom or any of its contents. She would have been right there in her bedroom, if not for divine intervention, and I would have never found her among all of the death and destruction. I shudder to think about how close she came to staying, and I thank God that she left. Had I listened to and followed my instincts, I would have left the coast with her on Sunday evening, and not thought twice about rather or not I would have a job come Monday. The jobs that we do in life are nothing compared to the relationships that we make, and I am so very thankful for the relationship that I have with my daughter. We both came so very close to losing each other that weekend.

I have always heard that God uses ordinary people to do extraordinary things, and that we only need to be willing by faith to allow Him to use us. What happened there that day among all of us at the police department was nothing short of a miracle. The one strength that held us all together and safe was the hand of God. He was there, right there beside each of us, and I know exactly when He reached down and took us all in His hands. As I watched from behind the dispatch window, I saw the look on my Chief's face when he first peaked out the window and through the small opening left by the plywood that had been put up to protect the floor to ceiling lobby window. The look on his face and the sound of his voice both conveyed disbelief and a slight hint of fear. At that moment, when he knew the real danger we were all in, the words that he spoke softly and with deep sincerity were "Oh My God". I know, at that very instant, God answered his cry for help because I could feel the presence of divine power fill the room. It was a very real, warm and immediate presence like nothing I have ever known before that day. In the minutes that followed the Chief turning away from that front window, something miraculous happened without any coaching or guidance of any sort from any of us. All of us, every single one of us in that building that morning, were spontaneously circled together in that narrow hallway, holding hands and reciting the Lord's Prayer. There had been no call to order from anyone there, but without fail we were all right there together. The prayer was spoken out loud, without hesitation or fumbling of words on anyone's part and every single word of it was said, from beginning completely to the very end. Grown adults, facing certain death, came together without prior calling and prayed the Lord's Prayer from the first word to the very last without any mess ups. God was most certainly there and had already taken full charge of our fates. Of all the words that my big, burly, Southern, good ole boy Chief of Police could have said when he first saw that wall of water coming toward us, he chose to call on the name of the Lord. He saved us all in that very instant, I have no doubt. Without God fully present there that day with us, none of us could have survived what came next. Six and a half hours fighting the full fury of Hurricane Katrina was a trial that tested us all, and many, many of us who may not have had a personal relationship with God before then most certainly witnessed His power and saving grace that day. Rather we deserved His helping hand or not is not for any of us to judge, but I can tell you from my first hand experience that He was there. Things happened so quickly the moment the last word of that prayer was out of our mouths, but for that moment in time while we prayed, time, and the fury of the storm and fear stood still. I will always be grateful that God put me in a place of employment that had a man of faith in charge, and I will always be grateful to my Chief for calling for God's help on that morning that Katrina made landfall.

I'm getting ahead of myself here, so let me back up to that weekend leading up to August 29, 2005. It was my weekend off work, and as much as I loved being a police dispatcher, I lived for those long weekends off. There was always something fun to do in the area around where I lived, and my friends and I also kept the highway hot between the Bay and Slidell, LA. Slidell had a daiquiri shop that we frequented, and there was also a little juke joint hidden way down on the salt bayou that we never missed a chance to go to. The daiquiri shop was just a stopping point for a little liquid encouragement to help us find our way down to that little bar and dance hall. I was only off from the PD every other weekend, so I had to make the best of the time I had. My friends and I already suspected that my weekend might be cut short due to the approaching hurricane, so we were bound and determined to make the most of the time we had.

It was Friday evening and the sun was just beginning to sink from the sky when we all met down on Beach Boulevard in Old Town Bay St. Louis. There was a group of us, from all walks of life and from all ages and stages, and we met together on the lower patio deck of one of the local beach bars to discuss the week that was ending and to watch the sunset. We relaxed and laughed together, sharing a little food and drink and lots of good company and conversation. I sat around the patio table with a group of women friends as they made their final list for the cruise they would be taking on September 10th. It was Friday night, August 26, 2005. The air was thick and heavy, and a breeze coming across the Gulf of Mexico was hard to come by that evening. The music played loud and free, and all was right with the world and deep within me. I had come to the area for healing and restoration of my spirit after the demise of a 25 year marriage, and over the course of four years, I had regained my self worth and genuine joy. Good friends . . . . a good job that never felt like work to me, and peace of mind and personal fulfillment—I found it all, every day, consistently day after day, right there in the Bay. My daughter had just recently come back to live with me, and my son and future daughter-in-law had both taken wonderful jobs in Las Vegas after traveling for more years than I cared to remember. All was right with the world for me, and life was good. I was genuinely, completely happy as I passed the time laughing and relaxing and visiting with friends, taking time to speak briefly with all those I knew who drifted in, and smiling at everyone I hadn't yet met. People . . . both strangers and friends gathered together in our little spot of paradise welcoming the weekend in.

Two of the officers I worked with were on the deck that night and we greeted each other with friendly hugs and toasted to the good times we shared when out of uniform. We exchanged casual comments in a joking way about enjoying the night that we had as it might be our last in light of that "monster" brewing out in the Gulf. We had heard all the weather reports but it all still seemed so far away. The three of us, Salty, and the retired postman turned cop and I, peered out into the darkness of the night sky and raised our glasses high . . . . "Here's to the good times"! None of us could dream how what was to come would change everything. We were carefree and young in spirit that night, simply out to laugh a little and wash our cares away.

Early in the evening, all the women in our group decided to call it a day—except for one friend and me. She and I said our goodbyes to the others and decided to visit another local nightspot there on the beach front. The Good Life was a favorite for those who enjoy karaoke, and although neither of us sings, we were always sure to have a good time there because of all the friends we would meet and greet. That Friday night was no different—the joint was packed! It wasn't long and our table was full of friends there for all the same reasons we were . . . good music, good conversation and pure relaxation. For that Friday night, all was right in our little piece of heaven along the Gulf coast—life was *more* than good in Bay/Waveland, MS.

Sometime around Midnight or 1AM I decided to call it a night and said goodbye to all of my friends. I didn't go straight home that evening. I drove up Main Street to the main highway through town and stopped to fill my truck up and talk a minute with the store clerk. As a night shift dispatcher, I had learned to appreciate those of us who work the long, dark hours while the rest of the world sleeps. Sometimes there are nights when we ache to see another's face and hear a sweet, kind word or two in the middle of the night. Tonight our smiles were forced and our words were encouraging and hopeful as we spoke of the monster storm out in the Gulf. For those of us who make our lives along the water's edge, that is the way for us . . . . cautious, yet hopeful with each new hurricane. Never knowing exactly where it will make landfall, and continually praying that it won't be us, yet sincerely hoping that it won't hit our neighbors either. From a distance, I know that others have a hard time understanding what makes us build our homes and our lives in harm's way—it seems silly, I know. But for those of us who live on the Gulf coast, there is no other way. The saltwater, the seagulls, the sunshine . . . . those are life sustaining necessities, and without them, we would merely exist without the full joy and passion for living that each of us is meant to experience. I don't expect everyone to understand. I simply tell you because for those of us who live on the coast, there is no other way.

TRY TO UNDERSTAND ~ THERE IS NO OTHER WAY

FOR THOSE OF YOU WHO DARE TO ASK WHY WE STAY
WHEN SALT WATER RUNS DEEP IN YOUR VEINS
AND EACH SEA BIRD SQUALKS OUT YOUR NAME . . .
THERE IS NO OTHER WAY.

WHEN YOU GAZE OUT UPON THE HORIZON
AND LONG TO SEE THE OTHER SIDE,
BREATHING IN BOTH THE OCEAN AND THE SKY,
SO FAR AND DEEP AND WIDE.

WHEN YOU ACHE FOR THE SOUND OF THE CRASHING WAVES
OR THE SOFT GENTLE WHISPERS OF THE FOAM KISSING THE
SAND
AND QUIETLY SLIPPING AWAY . . .
THERE IS NO OTHER WAY.

WHEN THE SUN BECKONS YOU TO COME OUT AND PLAY
AND THE MOON SOOTHES YOU AT THE END OF EACH DAY . . .
THERE IS NO OTHER WAY.

WHEN IT'S DEEP DOWN IN YOUR SOUL—
YOU CAN NOT LEAVE AND JUST SIMPLY WALK AWAY
YOU SIMPLY CANNOT LET IT ALL GO . . .
THERE IS NO OTHER WAY.

WE STAY, PLEASE TRY TO UNDERSTAND . . .
SIMPLY BECAUSE,
THERE IS NO OTHER WAY FOR US

I said goodnight to the store clerk and headed home. I took the long way home that night . . . . South on Hwy. 90 to the Bay Bridge and then turned right onto Beach Blvd. The moon was out that night and casting its reflection on the smooth water, making it shimmer like glass in the hot, sticky, quiet night. The hush was almost deafening with the stillness that lurked that night, and the air was thick and heavy. I noticed as I drove past the huge trees that hang out over the roadways there that even the featherweight Spanish moss draped delicately over the tree branches seemed to be weighting them down. Those huge tree branches seemed to be tired and old tonight, almost as though the heaviness of the humidity in the night air and the darkness of the midnight hours were too much to bear. I can't explain exactly what I was feeling that night, but something was different . . . not quite right . . . and it seemed as though even the trees could feel it in the air. Those gorgeous Southern mansions that are thick along the roadway there stood proud and braced looking out over the Bay, as though they held a breathless stare far beyond what my eyes could see.

It's somehow now, as though they knew that this was no ordinary hurricane but one like none of us had ever seen. The walls of those old mansions could always talk. One could always hear the history of the area if they simply looked and listened. The pirates who sought shelter from the sea must have been frequent and many, and the runaways who hid out from whomever or whatever they ran from spent time here too, I feel quite sure. And the men who sought refuge along this shoreline were surely never alone, for the houses were each and every one full of giggling, and anxious to please and satisfy their needs "ladies of the night", to put it nicely. You could feel the history of this area just by standing in its presence.

This quaint little town, hidden safely along the shoreline of one of the many bays that dip inland from the Gulf of Mexico, truly was "a place set apart" from the rest of this world. It was home to many of us, not merely by our street addresses, but profoundly deep in our souls. It was my home. The place that I found total peace and fulfillment deep in my soul, and although many miles separated me, I somehow felt closer to my family and friends, closer to my God there than I had felt in many, many years. It was for me, a healing place. That place beside the still waters where He restores my soul. My spirit was alive there. My faith was strong and sure there. My joy was overflowing there. It was my home there.

As I drove the curve of the roadway and took in the beauty of the night, I remember talking to God as I let the truck idle slowly along at its own pace. I recalled all the many blessings of my life and smiled softly as I thanked Him, and I shut my eyes tight in reverence as I pleaded for His safety and security during whatever was yet to come. I remember confessing that I was a little worried about what was happening out in the Gulf, but in that same breath I remember acknowledging that I was not feeling *afraid* because I KNOW with God I need not fear anything. Psalm 57:1 came to mind for me that night ~ ~ ~ ***Have mercy on me O God . . . for in you my soul takes refuge. I will take refuge in the shadow of your wings until the disaster has passed.*** Yet the uneasiness was there within me and I struggled with it, admitting to God of that uneasiness, and also of the guilt I felt for even feeling it! I know that I know that I *KNOW* that God protects and holds each of us in His hands, but *this* was a "monster hurricane" and I was a little worried. I talked to God that night as I traveled home by way of Beach Boulevard, and that conversation never ceased and continues, still, even today. I am not ashamed to admit that over the next few days following this Friday night, I felt very, very afraid, and still am fearful of things somewhat to a certain degree even today. I will tell you also, that even in the midst of the storm and now in its aftermath, my assurance and hope and faith is much stronger than my fear. God never gives us more than we can handle, and He equips us with all that we need to handle things that we have never imagined we might ever be faced with. Yea though I walk through the valley of death I will fear no evil, for thy rod and thy staff they comfort me . . . God is always with us. He *always has* and *still does* comfort and protect us. After experiencing such destruction and devastation left by Hurricane Katrina, I have found my *home*. When I stand at my former street address and see no traces of my home left, I find it in that *every day, continual* conversation with God. Store not your treasures up here on Earth, my friend . . . bury them deep within your heart and carry them with you always.

It was Saturday morning and I had planned to sleep in. After all, it would probably be a busy few days with the threat of the lurking hurricane so I'd better be rested and ready for what was to come. Little did I know, nor could I have ever imagined what was to come! The phone rang around 11am, piercing abruptly through the quietness of the morning. I fumbled from my bed to answer it, and it was the call that I had been anticipating and dreading both. It was the Chief advising that we were officially on "standby" for the pending emergency that the hurricane had produced.

For the remainder of the weekend, right up until I reported for my shift on Sunday evening at 6PM, I prayed and watched the weather channel. I ran through the important things concerning my life in my mind, and I called and spoke with several friends and family members just to let them know that I would be okay with the PD, and to tell them that I loved them. Any fears that I had turned to a quiet determination and a peaceful feeling deep inside, just in case I didn't make it through this alive.

CHAPTER 2

THE DAY ~ ~ AUGUST 29, 2005

My Sunday night shift was relatively quiet, without emergencies, but with only a few phone calls from concerned citizens who had decided to stay on the coast in their homes. They ask the strangest questions when they called in the middle of that night, but mostly it was the same question over and over again: "Do you think it's going to hit us?" The winds had kicked up to about 75mph after Midnight Sunday night, and the rain was gusting in intermittent sheets with the wind. Hurricane Katrina was still out in the Gulf waters and classified as a category 4 hurricane. She was big and bad, true enough, but at that point it seemed as though she were headed straight for New Orleans. Although Waveland would feel the outer bands of wind and rain, we would be alright if she stayed on that course. LORD, I wish I had known to tell them . . . . to warn those who called me that night, and to *insist* that they leave the area. But then, the weather channel had been warning us all, and I think so many of those callers felt like surely it would be okay to stay if the police department was staying. God, I wish we had left. We *should have* moved out of our building and away from the coast on Saturday when the Civil Defense left the area. I thought all along that they were still there on the coast with us, and it was not until 4:30am Monday morning that I learned different. I was shocked and truly angry when I ask my Assistant Chief about where the Civil Defense was waiting out the storm, and when our department was going to move to a safer location. He answered in what almost sounded to me to be a snickering tone of voice . . . . "They pulled out of here on Saturday. We are the only emergency agency still left down here". I could not believe what I was hearing, and my immediate response to him was "Well, what in the hell are we still doing here? When do ya'll plan to move us?" He knew I was upset and all he could do was hang his head and tell me that it was too late for us to try to move. It was at that moment, at 4:30am that Monday morning as Hurricane Katrina made her way N/NW in the Gulf, that I became afraid and angry. The Chief had promised that we would move to a safe place and come back in after the hurricane passed, but now I knew that he had no intention of making sure we would be as safe as possible. The Assistant Chief told me that the Mayor had refused to let the Chief send the police department employees out of harm's way, but instead, had insisted that our job was to protect and serve and we would no longer have a job if we decided to leave the area. The City Of Waveland had decided to play roulette with my life against a predicted killer storm, and I was never even asked if I wanted to participate as a player. My name . . . . my life, was put in jeopardy simply for the sake of the Chief and Mayor's egos. I was on the wrong city payroll at the wrong time, and my life had been bet against some pretty rough odds.

By 5:30am, all the day shift officers had arrived at the station. They had spent the night at a local hotel just down the highway from the police station. They reported that the rain was blowing into the rooms under the doors, and the wind was so strong that they could hardly make it to the patrol cars when they left the rooms. Those of us who had worked all night, decided to stay at the PD with everybody else rather than going to that hotel. That decision helped save our lives, as the entire bottom floor of the hotel was completely washed away by the hurricane, and we would have been swept away by the tidal surge had we been sleeping there. For the next several hours, we all remained in the station, watching the weather channel and listening to the wind and rain pounding outside. We still believed, at that point, that the worst of the hurricane would spare us in Waveland, MS. It still appeared to be heading directly for New Orleans, and did, in fact, initially cross land in South Louisiana near Buras. We watched on the television as it made landfall there, and at that moment, we all breathed a little sigh of relief. It was somewhere around 8:30am when I phoned my daughter in Memphis to let her know that I would be okay and would call her as soon as I could after everything was over. I hung the phone up and said a quiet, cautious prayer of thanks.

By 9am, our incoming phone lines at the PD began to light up . . . . every line was ringing. We first thought that the phones were going out, but quickly realized that they were lit up with incoming calls. I stepped up to help the day dispatcher answer some of the lines, and our Chief also reached across the desk to pick up a ringing line. People were saying things that we couldn't understand. They were talking about water entering there homes and asking us to help them get out. We were trying to take names and addresses from the callers when our phone lines went down. We were confused about those last phone calls.

There was a very brief time that morning, as the water began to fill the building that I remember a moment of panic. It seemed to hit us all at the same time. Water was between our ankles and our knees, and I think all of us realized in the same instant just how fast it was rising and filling our building up. A night sergeant ran down the hall through the water to the back door, and many of us instinctively followed him hoping to exit the building that way. A patrol car had already floated and lodged itself against the door, and it would not open. Realizing we were trapped inside the building, we turned and ran as best we could through the rising water toward the front of the building. The electrical box and all the electronic computer and radio equipment components were in a small room parallel to the dispatch office, and the water was filling that room up. I saw our Chief step up onto a rolling office chair and reach for the electrical power switch on the far wall of that room. I remember hearing yelling and screaming and feeling several officers lunge for him. We thought that he would surely be electrocuted, and the officers snatched him away before he touched the metal box. The phones had stopped ringing and the weather channel was silent on a black television screen. We realized that our building had lost power, and you could hear our relief as we released the fear of being electrocuted. I recalled those last phone calls . . . . the sounds of panic and despair in the voices of the people gripped with fear. Their cries for help were desperate and pleading, and left us confused for the first few moments. That's when our Chief went to the lobby and peaked through the tiny openings left by the plywood covering the plate glass windows. He was the first to see the huge wall of water thundering toward us. I will never forget the look of disbelief on his face or the sound of both fear and reverence in his voice as I heard him cry out "Oh My God"! The height of the tidal surge was so great that the solid wall of water was visible as it overtook the entire shopping center directly across the highway from our building. The wall of water was topped with 5' to 6' waves with white caps as it rolled toward us. Fierce, intense, ferocious . . . . Mother Nature in her full force and glory. I realized in that instant what those people making those last phone calls had seen and experienced. My heart cried out in fear for all of us, and with compassion for those already engulfed by her.

CRYING OUT FOR GRACE

AS I WATCHED HIM PEER OUT OF THE FRONT WINDOW,
I COULD SEE IT ALL OVER HIS FACE.
I HEARD IN HIS VOICE THE REVERENCE AS HE WHISPERED
"OH MY GOD", AS THOUGH BEGGING FOR GOD'S GRACE . . .

IN AN INSTANT WE WERE ALL GATHERED AROUND IN A CIRCLE,
OUR SPIRITS JOINED TIGHT BY OUR HANDS.
IN UNISON AND WITHOUT HESITATION,
CAME EVERY WORD OF THE LORD'S PRAYER . . .
SPOKEN OUT LOUD, BY EVERY WOMAN AND EVERY MAN.

WE COULD SCARCELY GET THE WORDS OUT
BEFORE THE WATERS CAME RUSHING IN,
THE WINDS SCREAMED AROUND OUR BUILDING,
AND THE WALLS BEGAN TO CREAK AND BEND.

WE FELT TRAPPED AND COULD NOT BREATH . . .
WE MADE THE DECISION TO LEAVE.
A CHAIR THROUGH THE LOBBY WINDOW,
AND POUNDING THE PLYWOOD UNTIL IT GAVE WAY . . .
WATER CAME RUSHING IN AND SWEPT SEVERAL OF US AWAY.

WE FRANTICALLY SCRAMBLED,
AND GATHERED EVERYONE TOGETHER AGAIN . . .
ONE BY ONE OUR JOURNEY BEGAN.
HOLDING TIGHT TO EACH OTHER,
WE FORMED A HUMAN CHAIN
HOLDING EACH OTHERS HANDS.

SOME WENT TO THE HIGHWAY AND CLUNG TO THE BUSH
SOME RODE IT OUT ON THE BACK OF A TRUCK.
OTHERS BARELY MADE IT OUT OF THE BUILDING,
AND WERE CAUGHT BY THE FORCE OF
THE WATER WHERE THEY WERE.

THERE WERE A FEW CLINGING TO THE FLAGPOLE,
AND SOME NEAR THE BUILDING'S ROOF.
A MIRACLE UNFOLDED THERE THAT MORNING,
AND ALL TWENTY-EIGHT OF US ARE THE PROOF.

I remember the feeling of that first forceful flush of tidal surge as it came flooding through the lobby and completely overtook our building. It sent us all flailing and fighting to catch our breath, and frantically grabbing and screaming as it swept us off our feet. In every direction, and all down the hallway, it flung us and threw us and pinned some against the walls. It felt like certain death even then. We reached for each other, holding on to whomever we could. We formed a human chain linking hands together, and locking in our promises to not leave each other behind . . . not even one. As we started through that broken lobby window, fighting against what seemed to me to be impossible odds, many of us cried. We were the leaders in times of need, yet we all realized that this time it was us who were seriously in need. I remember distinctly hearing the Chief's secretary cry out in genuine fear to her husband, who is an investigator with the department, as they helped each other out into the open where the storm was in its full fury. Her voice shook and was filled with fright as she held onto him so tight, knowing she could not swim and this might very well be the end for her. Her normal, jovial self, that I had come to know and love, had disappeared and left her like a small, frightened little girl. My heart broke for all of us as I faced what I most certainly thought was the impossible. I thought at that moment that we would all surely die. There was no shame in witnessing a grown man or woman cry that morning. Brave, and almost always in control, we all became like scared, lost children that day. To feel the warmth and the comfort of those we loved and the security of our own homes at that moment was a prayerful pleading from many of us, I am sure. My thoughts were on those that I love, as I feel sure was on so many other's minds too. It was magnified and revived deep inside many of us that day, how it's not the stuff that we collect along the way, but rather the relationships that we nurture each day that really matters in life. I'm so thankful that the men and women of Waveland PD were not only police officers, but more importantly friends who vowed to hold on to each other that day. Each of us was willing to do whatever it would take to make sure that not a single one of us would die that day. We were truly brothers and sisters that morning, in the exact and full way that I believe God wants us to be always. John 15:13 . . . . No greater love has a man than to lay down his life for his brother.

At the height of the tidal surge, and in the worst kind of wind that you cannot even begin to imagine, I can remember opening my eyes and feeling the salt water stinging them so badly that I could barely see anything. I turned around to see if the waters were still coming at us even deeper than they already were, and I could see a shrimp boat being tossed about near Hwy. 90 on top of the bank . . . . on TOP of the bank building! I could see the entire contents of the pharmacy and other stores being pushed out of the buildings and swept away with the raging waters. Entire building walls were being flung about, and rooftops and tin and bricks were flying all around us like missiles. The thought of being decapitated by flying debris crossed my mind and I held on tight and continued to pray. The vehicles were turning over and over and bobbing about like tiny toys in a bathtub. I could feel the truck I was standing on floating and swaying side to side as though it was going to roll upside down at any moment. I held on tight and continued to pray. Surviving the terror of that day was nothing short of a miracle, and I still have nightmares about it to this very day.

About three hours into the fight for survival against this hurricane, I felt my left shoulder pulling out of place, and my fingers cramped and ached from the death grip I had on the light bar on the roof of the truck I was holding on to. I struggled to try to relax my body enough so as to concentrate on calming my mind, which was filled with the deafening sounds of my silent screams. I was being completely covered up by the raging waters now, and I felt the certainty of near death for the first real time since this whole ordeal had begun. I saw my children's faces in my minds eye, and I spoke softly to each of them as I whispered a sweet and gentle goodbye. I could feel myself struggling to twist and pull away from the other officers there with me. They were holding me to keep me from being swept away, and I was fighting for them to let me go. The pain in my shoulder was sharp and burned hot even in the freezing cold waters. I was stretched as high as I could go while still holding on, and the water was even higher than that as it covered me up completely. I waited, trying not to panic, and I held my breath. The water did not subside, and I felt its grip not only on my body, but also consuming my mind. The truck was rocking violently and twisting and turning with the force of the raging water. I panicked and I struggled to find a breath of air. I stretched upward higher and higher, afraid to let go of the light bar, knowing that I would be swept away in the surge. I prayed for another breath of life if for no other reason than to be able to die in peace, and I felt my left shoulder pulling and stretching as I strained to get my head above the water. I tried desperately to calm my mind as my body fought harder and harder to survive. Drowning is such a terrible way to die because your body fights against it so fiercely, and your mind searches for peace as you try to prepare yourself to die. In the instant that I was ready to give up the fight and give in to dying, I saw my Mother's eyes. It was not her whole face there before me, but just her tear filled eyes and her sad, wrinkled brow. I never heard her speak a word, but I understood why she was there all the same. She did not call my name and yet I could hear the sweet sound of her voice completely and totally throughout my entire mind and body. That's when I knew that I had to hang on and continue the fight. Somehow, like a miracle, I felt the water running off my face and I tasted drops of salt water in my mouth. Although my entire body was still held tight in the grips of the raging, deep waters, my lips were just barely above it enough to allow me to take a deep, gasping breath of air. At that point I wanted to live. I wanted to find a way to survive what seemed to me to be against impossible odds.

For a Mother to lose a child of any age in life just is not right. The order of our lives is that we accept the sadness of burying our parents, not that a parent should have to bury a child. The bond between a Mother and her child defies all worldly time lines and remains eternal in the deepest part of her heart. When her child dies, a part of her also dies with them. My own children could have wept and grieved my passing and somehow found their strength to go on to live their lives, but my Mother very possibly would not have been able to do that. I knew she had come to be with me in that darkest moment of fear in order to give me the strength I needed to hang on. I have never feared death, but My Oh My, how very much sweeter is life! Deep in my heart and engraved in my mind, I will always and forever remember my Mother's eyes.

MY MOTHER'S EYES

WE ALL FOUGHT TOGETHER, YET EACH ON HIS OWN
BOUND TIGHT WITH THE PROMISE *NOT TO LET GO*!
THE WATERS SWELLED FAST AND SWEPT BY US
WITH SUCH RAGE . . . THE WINDS ROARED AND
HOWLED 'ROUND US, CREATING CHAOS AND
CRASHING WAVES. IT HAPPENED SO FAST AND YET
WE THOUGHT IT'D NEVER END. THERE WAS NOT
ONCE A CEASE OR LULL IN THE SWIRLING WATERS
AND SCREAMING WINDS.

I SAW MY CHILDREN'S FACES, WITH TEARS AS THEY
TOLD ME GOODBYE . . . I SHOULD HAVE ~ ~ I VERY
EASILY COULD HAVE DIED . . . AND THEN I SAW MY
MOTHER'S EYES. SUCH STRENGTH AND YET FILLED
WITH SORROW AS SHE PAINFULLY WATCHED ME SLIP
AWAY. SEEING THE ANGUISH OF A MOTHER LOSING
HER CHILD GAVE ME STRENGTH TO CONTINUE TO
FIGHT TO SEE ANOTHER DAY.

SOMEONE ASK IF I'D SEEN MY DAD DURING
THAT TIME OF TRAUMA . . . I DIDN'T AND *NOW* I
UNDERSTAND WHY . . . LIFE IS FOR THE LIVING ~ I
COULD SEE THAT IN MY MOTHER'S EYES.

I'M SURE MY DAD WAS THERE . . . PERHAPS
SOMEWHERE OUT OF SITE. IF I HAD SEEN OR FELT
HIM, I WOULD NOT HAVE CONTINUED TO FIGHT
FOR MY LIFE. THE COMFORT OF HIS ARMS AND THE
STRENGTH OF HIS LOVE WOULD HAVE ALLOWED ME
TO SURRENDER AND JOIN HIM ABOVE.

LIFE IS FOR THE LIVING AND *SO* WORTH
THE FIGHT ~ ~ ~ I AM SO GRATEFUL
THAT I COULD SEE THAT IN MY MOTHER'S EYES.

DECEMBER 2005 ~ CDS

The instant that I locked eyes with that officer on the rooftop, I felt my body being hurled through the raging waters and swept toward the front of the building. I felt a hand reach out and grab hold of me and pull me up close near the flagpole. There were two of my officers hanging on to that flagpole. I had worked with them both on the night shift for several years, and I could hear both of them comforting me. As they wrapped the loose end of the flagpole rope around my wrist and secured my hands around it tightly, I could hear their words of reassurance that we were all going to be alright. I heard that young country boy from up in the Kiln whisper sincerely to me "Hang on Mama, we are going to get you to safety". That young boy became a real man in my eyes that day. He helped me focus on surviving and calmed me enough to be able to do that. I felt them let me go as they yelled "Hang On!", and I clung to the rope while it carried me to the far right side of the rooftop of the building. There was a small wooden section of roof about 3 or 4 feet below the tin roof of the PD that was built to cover a generator, and it became my anchor as I struggled to keep from being swept away. I felt myself being pulled up on that shaky, wooden structure and was able to see at least four or five officers holding on to my clothes and struggling with all they had left in them to get me up on that roof. Finally, FINALLY, I felt my body being rolled onto the ruff shingles and into the arms of what felt like safety to me. There were others who had reached that roof before me and together we helped each one up to the tin roof of the PD in order to make room for the rest to come. The tin roof was wet and cold and hard under our bellies as we stretched out face down and covered our heads with our arms to keep the flying debris from decapitating us. That tin roof creaked and popped and groaned underneath us as the ferocious wind threatened time and again to rip it apart out from under us. It felt to me as though the building was buckling under the pressure of the tidal surge, and I could feel the roof lifting up by the force of the wind. I laid there frozen in shock and fear, and I prayed. Over and over again I prayed. Continuously, without ceasing or forethought,

I heard the scriptures and prayers pouring out of me. From the deepest, darkest corners of my mind, the light began to shine through as all of my Christian upbringing began to surface. As I laid in that certain valley of death, Psalms 23 poured out from my soul and directly into the heart of my Heavenly Father. Every bible verse and nursery rhyme song that I had ever heard came forth from me that day. Words and promises from God that I couldn't remember having even ever heard . . . . they were all there in my hour of need. "Bring up a child in the way he should go and when he is old he will not depart from it" took on new meaning for me that day. I now understand why my Mother and Father had struggled so hard and tirelessly through the years to make sure we were in church and connected to a Christian family. My sister and brother and I were encouraged to be active participants in our church family, not just children who were sent to the cry room during the sermons or allowed to sleep on the pew. I know now why God tells us to store up His word in our hearts, because for me, on that day, it was my anchor and my beacon of hope as I struggled to stay alive, all the while watching as so many others died. I'm not trying to imply that God took any special favor with me that day, but I can tell you that He would have had to stop all else in order to be able to pry me away from Him during that storm. There was nothing to physically hang on to keep myself on that roof during some of the worst hours of that storm, but for three and a half more hours I clung to Him and He never let me go. I believe being a Christian made all the difference for me that day, and I encourage others to join with me in finding and maintaining that same kind of difference in their own lives. Some say we are wrong about our faith in God and that we won't know it for sure until the time that we die, but for me, He made all the difference in saving my life that day.

To be completely honest, I can't remember much about those last 3 or 4 hours I spent on the roof. What I can recall, and may never overcome, is the sound of the winds and the sting of the needle sharp rain. At some point, even those memories fade and I can only recall hearing my own prayers. I remember that although I could not speak, I could plainly hear and feel my prayers and long forgotten scriptures and bible verses pouring out of me. It was as though a thin plastic bubble surrounded me. I could feel it being stretched and pulled violently away from me as though it would tear away and snatch my body away with it. Inside that bubble, frozen as still as I could lie, I talked to God. Not in a worldly, educated Christian way, but in a sincere, heartfelt child of God way. He knew my needs and I knew my Savior. He heard my cries and I let go of all control. I pleaded for my safety and I let His promises and praises flow. All the Christian truths that I had ever been taught . . . . all the bible verses I had ever memorized and all the Sunday school nursery rhythms that I'd ever sang . . . . they all came pouring, *no, flooding* out of me that day. God heard my cries. He heard my needs. God put a bubble of protection from the storm completely around me that day.

Just as soon as the winds stopped howling and screaming, and the waters started to flow rapidly back into the bay, we started looking for a place of safety out of the storm. I was still laying face down on the tin roof of the police department building, and still had my arms covering my head as protection from flying debris. I felt my lieutenant shaking my leg and telling me to "Come on Ms. Denise. We are going to get down from here. We are going to be okay now." I could feel my head rise up to look at him, and I heard myself talking to him. It was only my imagination responding to him. I could not move my body, or even speak. I was frozen with fear, lying there on that rooftop, and numb with shock. I wanted to get off that roof and get to a safe place, but I could not move. I remember tasting salt water and thinking that I must have drowned and was only dreaming about safety. I wonder now if it were my own tears that I tasted. I remember feeling an arm slip across my back and around my waist, and I could hear a soft voice assuring me that he was going to help me and we were going to be okay. It was my lieutenant, laying on his belly on that cold, wet roof right there beside me and comforting me with his kind, reassuring words. He promised to stay right there with me and help me scoot to the edge of the roof so we could get down. His courage and patience helped to relax me enough to allow him to help me. He never left my side and he scooted on his stomach, same as I had to do. I was numb with fear and exhausted, but together we managed to inch our way slowly but surely to the edge of the roof. There were several officers standing just below us on the small wooden roof covering the generator. As soon as the lieutenant and I were within reach, they grabbed hold of us and helped us down to the roof they were standing on. My knees buckled under me and I slid down on that rooftop with my back leaning up against our office building. I could still hear the tremendous noise of the winds and the thunderous rumbling of the raging waters. Again, it was just my imagination. The winds had died down to probably 50 to 60 miles per hour by this time, and the water had subsided leaving only about 5' still swirling around us. When I was finally able to realize that, I was filled with the faith and hope of coming out of this nightmare alive. We debated how to get down from that rooftop and make our way to safety. There was still water all around us, and it was churning and rapidly being pulled back out into the bay. To jump the 10 to 12 feet from where we were down into that water would surely have been suicide for some of us. We had to find another way to get down. I remember seeing a couple of officers coming through the water across the highway with a small, flat bottom john boat, but I'm not sure why that wasn't used to help us. Then, without hesitation, two of our police officers jumped into the water and struggled against its force enough to swim to some storage buildings next door to the PD. They went under the water several times trying to open the doors on many of the storage units. They finally were able to find one that would open, and inside that storage room they found a tall ladder. The ladder reached the roof we were standing on, and we began to climb down, one by one. Before each of us reached the water, there were two more officers waiting below us to help keep us from getting carried away with the receding tidal surge. Three at a time, with arms locked together at our elbows, we helped each other make our way through the water and out onto the highway median. We were half running and half being pushed along by the strong winds, as well as being dragged by the force of the water rushing back out to sea. I felt so close to being safe finally, and yet we were all still so far from it. I don't remember which two officers I walked away from there with that day, but I thank them and am grateful to them for not letting me slip away. We crossed the highway, still in waist deep water, and made our way down a side street where we could see a house on dry land. The people in that house handed us dry towels to wipe the salt water from our wind burnt faces, and offered us fresh water to drink. We had survived the hurricane, and as we stood together there under that carport, we hugged each other and cried. All of us, every last one of us was alive. Nothing short of a miracle had occurred at our police department that day. There is no human explanation as to how and why, but all 28 of us had survived. It wasn't long after that when we saw a school bus being driven by Bay PD Assistant Chief on the highway directly in front of the house where we were. We all ran to the bus and climbed aboard, exhausted and still feeling the fear of the whole ordeal. The bus stopped several times to pick up others who had survived. Everyone looked shocked and in a daze. We finally reached the Civil Defense building in the Bay. When I stepped off that bus, I could still feel the force of the winds and water that had come so close to taking my life that day. I knew I had finally reached a safe place, but my mind and my body were still reeling from the force of the hurricane. I made my way up the front steps and into the building, and that is where I took shelter for the next three days and nights. On that Thursday, after the hurricane had come through the previous Monday, I walked out of there into the waiting arms of my daughter and my brother. They had traveled a long way and overcome a lot of obstacles to reach the coast, but they had found a way to come get me. I was dirty and still wet down to my bones, but seeing those two made me feel safe and like I was finally home. Numb with shock, and with a deep, heavy sadness inside of me, I stepped into the backseat of the car and we shut the doors and drove away. I've gone back there a few times, and I've missed it every day . . . . but I thank God that I survived it and was able to walk away.

CHAPTER 3

The Day After ~ ~ August 30, 2005

THE KNIGHTS ARRIVED IN CAMOUFLAGE

I can't remember for sure, because of the state of shock I was in I suppose, but I believe the first troop of National Guard soldiers arrived in Bay St. Louis late Tuesday night, August 30th. They arrived in the military vehicles and dressed from head to toe in camouflage uniforms. As they filed into the building where we had taken refuge, I felt several emotions overtaking me. I was so very proud that our military had come to our aid, and I also felt fear and confusion as they spoke of taking charge, marshal law and helicopters to rescue us all and shuttle us to shelters at locations away from the devastated coastline. As these men began to open their cots and set up their sleeping quarters, I couldn't help but notice that so very many of them were mere boys . . . . younger than my own son, and yet for all appearances they were acting as seasoned older men. They appeared to be very disciplined and professional as they quietly made their presence known. They were there on a mission to save us and to take over full control of the situation facing them. Although I was glad they were there with us, I also felt fear and confusion. I did not want to be under the control of the military, and I certainly did not want to be forced to board a helicopter and taken to some unknown location. I was scared and lonesome, and I remember feeling like a little girl who was lost from her Mother and filled with panic and fright. I think I sat quietly huddled on the floor, with my back against the wall and cried softly. I felt so lost and alone . . . . I was physically and emotionally exhausted as I sat there and cried and prayed. When all the movement and confusion in the room settled down, I stopped crying and raised my head to look around. At a table across the room, I saw a woman dressed in her military uniform. I watched her setting up a table with what appeared to me to be radio equipment. Her eyes met mine and she smiled at me. My eyes averted downward away from hers, afraid of revealing my fear and the fact that I had been crying. I felt ashamed . . . . I was a grown woman, a 911 police dispatcher, and I felt ashamed that I was crying. Being a woman in charge, I think she understood and she kept working and didn't push me to talk. Within the hour, she was there kneeling beside me and asking if I was okay. She ask if I had any family in the area, and when I told her that I did not, she offered to let me call someone on the military satellite phone. I cried again, so thankful for her compassion. I tried first to call my daughter in Memphis, but her cell phone was not working to receive my call. Hard as I tried, my mind was too jumbled to remember my son's phone number. Finally, I dialed my Mother's number and the call went through. It was late, almost midnight by now. When I heard my Mother answer, her voice sounded fragile and broken, and full of sadness to me. All I could say to her through my tears was "Mama, it's me. I am alive, and boy do I have a story to tell. Can somebody please come get me Mama?" I heard the relief in her voice as she first asked me if I was okay, and then exactly where I was. She assured me that they would come for me. I thanked that woman in charge of the military communication equipment, and returned to my spot against the wall to wait. I waited and I prayed, thanking God for the sound of my Mother's voice. I drifted in and out of a light sleep that night, shivering from my cold wet clothes, and weeping deep inside from the emptiness I felt deep in my soul. I couldn't wait to see the sunlight again. It was so very, very quiet and dark and still that first full night after the hurricane. No electrical power, no people and traffic, even the birds and other wildlife in the area were completely silent and still. There was such a profound, noticeable emptiness engulfing the entire area that night. It deepened my fear and loneliness, but I held on to the promise that I would soon be going home. I had heard my Mother's voice, and she had promised they would come for me.

On Tuesday morning, at the crack of dawn, I was anxious to make my way to Saint Charles Street to see the damage done to my house. An investigator with Waveland PD had borrowed someone's truck to get around in, as the entire department fleet of vehicles had been lost in the tidal surge. He offered to take me to my house, and I jumped at the chance. We stopped briefly at the Bay police department for me to get a dry t-shirt, and then we were on our way. I was excited to be going to see my neighborhood, but my joy turned to horror, increasing every inch of the way. Most roads were impassable. Debris of all sorts imaginable, along with dead people and animals were scattered everywhere. Everything had been destroyed and thrown about; coming to rest in stacks as high as 3 to 4 feet in most areas. Huge, ancient trees had been twisted around and around, and their trunks were snapped off near to the ground, leaving nothing but jagged splinters protruding from the earth. It looked to me like all the pictures I had ever seen of the aftermath of a nuclear bomb. Instead of being ash dry and smoking though, everything was dripping wet and stinking like mold and death. We could not make our way to Saint Charles Street in the truck, so we stopped in the roadway and he hailed me a ride on the back of a 4 wheeler. I had never in my life been on an ATV, but I stepped up on it and straddled behind the driver without hesitation. I had to see my house, my neighborhood, for myself. We could only drive as far as 2 blocks and were forced to park the ATV and walk through the rubble the rest of the way. At the intersection of Saint Charles and Third, my heart sank and I felt as though every drop of blood in my body had drained out of me. I was completely speechless and could hear myself screaming and crying, but there was not a sound or a tear coming out of me. The entire neighborhood was totally destroyed and lying in a tangled mess stacked solid and about four feet high. As I stood numb with shock and disbelief, the gentleman who had driven me there reached his hand out to comfort me, and he held me while I cried and struggled to keep my knees from buckling under me. Everything, for as far as our eyes could see, was broken and ruined and lay exposed in the streets. Our personal lives were strewn about, and although some things could be recognized such as ruined pictures and pieces of furniture, there was no possible way to begin to separate my things from all the rest. I could not begin to distinguish my personal things from anyone else's. No one would ever be able to fix this mess. I wept . . . . I prayed . . . . and I left.

Also on this day, I was able to get a full view of the total, mass destruction along Highway 90 throughout the Bay/Waveland area. The damage was unbelievable. It was indescribable. It was truly horrifying. Buildings that were left standing had been completely gutted by the raging waters of the tidal surge. Trees were stripped bare of all leaves, and most had been twisted at the huge trunks and snapped off at about three feet from the ground. So many of the giant trees were either laid over with the roots completely exposed, or they had been completely ripped from the ground and carried away so nothing was left but a deep, empty hole in the ground. Most of the broken tree trunks that remained standing were stripped bare of their bark and looked like a dwarf bush with thin wooden splinters sprouting out of the center of the trunk. In the parking lot of Waveland PD, vehicles had been tossed about, turned over and stacked on top of one another. One car was left delicately balanced on top of a grocery shopping cart when the waters subsided and returned to the Bay. There had most certainly been a battle along the coast on August 29, 2005 and Mother Nature had won hands down. The only defense we could have possibly engaged against her was to pack up and pull out before she arrived. The Chief and the Mayor decided against that and many of the city's first responders almost died. When it was over, we felt no shame in helping each other cry. Grown adults, brave men and women . . . . we all cried.

BROKEN AND BRUISED

So many have stories
That sound so profound
Those of us who were there
That day Katrina hit the ground

Her anger and fury
As she ravaged our land
Was worse than any of you can imagine
Not one of you possibly can

To be there in her grip
To experience it first hand
Caught in the center
Being squeezed by her hand

She managed to grab some
As she screamed and raged
For so very many of us
She simply left us in a daze

A numbness that remains
So deep in our souls

CHAPTER 4

ONGOING AFTERMATH AND SCATTERED THOUGHTS

A HERO OR AN ANGEL ~ ONE IN THE SAME

If there was one officer who showed himself to me to be any more of a hero than all the rest, it was the state highway patrolman who just happened to be working with us while waiting to go back to work for the state. When I was at my last bit of strength for staying above the water, and just when I was ready to surrender and was praying for my angels to come carry me home, he was there. I'm not sure if he had been clinging to that bush like so many others, or exactly where he had been before I saw him standing there . . . . atop the rooftop peak, struggling to stand against the unbelievably powerful force of the wind. He was cutting the rope from the flagpole as it whipped wildly around him, twisting and popping like a leather whip. I shudder even now to think how close he and I both came to death at that moment. I tremble in awe at my Heavenly Father's grace, and His power to use ordinary people to do extraordinary things. I believe that one of my angels that day was that officer on the rooftop. When I was finally able to open my eyes above the water again, for what I felt would be my last time before dying . . . . he was there, and he was the one thing that I could see clearly in all the chaos around me. His stature looked strong and stable as he stood on the edge of the peak of that roof, almost as though the wind and the rain and the howling tornadoes could not move him. I could see him looking at me and motioning for me to come that way. At that moment, I let go of that light bar. The death grip that I had held on with for almost 3 and ½ hours released instantly, and my eyes remained focused on him. Against all odds, and with almost no physical strength left in me, I was carried by the waters directly to the front of the submerged building right under where he stood. As I felt some other officers wrapping the rope from the flagpole around my wrist, I still never lost eye contact with my hero. I knew he was my angel who was there to help me survive that day. Although the sounds of the furious winds and waters around me were deafening, at that moment as I held the rope connecting the two of us, silence and calm and peace was all I was aware of for those few seconds. That's how I know for sure that he was the angel that God sent to me that day. Not a hero above any others, but an ordinary man allowing God to use him for an extraordinary purpose in our time of need. I say this, not to take credit away from any of the others who were there with our PD, for we were all heroes to each other in many extraordinary ways that day. I simply know that in what I thought would certainly be my last little bit of time left in this world, and as I prayed for God to send my angels to help me home, that officer was there, standing steady on the rooftop and motioning for me to trust him. Thank goodness that God did not answer that prayer from me, but instead chose to put that special officer there for me to see. God gave me a gift that day, and showed me the miracle of His power as He used that ordinary man to perform an extraordinary fete. Many, many miracles occurred that day, but for me personally, I believe this was the one, above all the rest, that saved my life. From now until forever, I will always see angel wings surrounding that officer when I visualize him standing on the peak of that rooftop.

Each new day is a gift from God

LEFT TO WONDER

There are still those I think about and wonder about their fates. People whom I encountered along the way, and slowed down just long enough to get to know. There's that cute, little Cajun man who twirled me round and round the dance floor and kept me giggling and playing like a little girl. I'll always wonder if he made it through this disaster. The woman I befriended when she would wait at our PD for her child custody exchange . . . I don't remember her name, but I will forever see her face and feel her kindness. She would always bring her special homemade holiday meals to me during Thanksgiving and Christmas when she knew I had to work. Then there was the gentleman who always watched out for me every other Sunday evening when I slipped off down by that bayou for a little rest and relaxation away from Waveland PD. He was a rough "biker type" guy on the outside, but a true, sincere gentleman, with a heart as pure as gold on the inside. I will always admire him for wanting to take care of me, and make sure no harm came my way. I pray they all made it through this okay.

It's because of people like these that I can be a better person. They opened my eyes and my heart to understand how very, very important it is to reach out and take someone else's hand.

None of us ever have to be alone in this world unless we choose to be. I have come to know that friendship is one of God's greatest gifts. It multiplies our joys and divides our sorrows when we share our life with friends.

My prayers go out to the families of those who did not survive. I will always remember them, especially as I stand at the seashore and gaze out upon the horizon. That particular view has always felt like what I imagine heaven will be for me. I will watch for their smiles and the twinkle in their eyes as I pray that I will see them all again someday.

God bless us all.

SOCIAL SECURITY SURPRISE

I doubt very seriously if I am the only American to misunderstand our social security system. What I thought I understood it to be was a "savings plan" of sorts, where I loaned the government part of every dollar I have ever earned and in turn, they held it in safe keeping for me and used it at their discretion for the betterment of our country until I needed it back. Low and behold, I was wrong! After almost a full year of struggling to rehabilitate myself back into the mainstream of life, I sought financial relief through my social security benefits that I have been socking away for times exactly like now since the very first paycheck that I have ever earned. I had read the requirements for being eligible for tapping into these funds, and I certainly met those guidelines. Social Security clearly states that we may draw our benefits earned prior to an injury when the injuries incurred render us unable to continue to perform the work duties that we were accustomed to doing. The trauma of the near drowning, along with the total loss of trust in my employer, has left me physically and emotionally unable to handle the duties required of a 911 operator. I believe, therefore, that I qualify for my social security disability benefits.

Obviously I'm misled in thinking that because our government branch of social security is doing it's best to disqualify me. This is not a government "handout" that I am seeking. I am simply asking for MY MONEY that I have deposited for THEIR BENEFIT all throughout the years that I have worked and earned a paycheck! It simply does not make sense to me how they can make accessing those personal funds so complicated and near impossible to recover in our time of need! It has been a very humbling and frustrating experience while trying to navigate our government's social security system.

I have faced the same type of scrutiny with worker's compensation insurance, and have been forced to attain legal representation regarding my needs and concerns for these benefits.

Amazing how I could have been so wrong in believing that I had some sort of security as a dedicated, dependable, hard working citizen, contributing to both a government and a city program that would help me in times of need, isn't it?

I have lost my faith through this ordeal in all levels of the system, from city and state, and all the way right on up to that big, white house on the hill.

Make no mistake, I am not discouraging faith and trust in our government, but merely sharing the fact that I have lost mine. I think our government believes that they have a working agenda in place to protect and serve the rights and the needs of every American. I have found those agendas too difficult to navigate, and far from "user friendly". I have been better suited through this whole ordeal with placing my faith and trust first in my God, then in my belief in myself and finally in the compassion and understanding of my family, friends and neighbors. That is how my needs were met during this time of crisis, not by my government with all of its agendas, but by my God and his children with all of their love for Him and each other.

One real concern that I have been left with after having to try to muddle through all the government red tape is our need as American citizens to do whatever it takes to simplify this maze. It is confusing, frustrating and infuriating! It takes as much time to navigate as a full-time job requires, and proves to be much more stressful and, more times than not, without benefit when the day is done. The government and many well known charitable organizations assure us that there are funds to help alleviate our losses, yet very few of us can access those funds. There are far too many obstacles and requirements throughout the entire application processes. I have a very strong opinion regarding this, and a deep desire to see changes made for the future, but quite frankly, I do not have the emotional or physical strength left in me to do much about it at this point. I have thrown my hands up in despair, and am attempting to go on with life.

ALL OF THE DONATIONS AND ALL OF THE HELP FROM OTHERS IN THIS WORLD DOES NOT ONE BIT OF GOOD IF WE THE PEOPLE WHO NEED THE HELP CANNOT RECEIVE IT BECAUSE OF THE CONFUSION AND RED TAPE FROM THE MIDDLE MAN WHOM IT IS ENTRUSTED TO.

The United States has a federal disaster assistance program set up to assist citizens in the event of a declared disaster. In my personal dealings with them over this past year, I have had my eyes opened wide to many inadequacies and much misuse of federal grant assistance funds.

THIS is what my home looked like after Hurricane Katrina. Officials from our federal disaster assistance program determined it to be "insufficient loss" for assistance.

FEMA inspectors denied assistance because they didn't think there was enough lost here! They have denied each and every appeal requesting re-determination. ABSURD, don't you think?

Our government financial assistance programs are so out of reason and messed up. I have seen it first hand for the first time in my life, and I am appalled. How does it happen that they can justify handing out $11,000.00 grants to some individuals who have never even worked long enough to earn that much income, or paid an insurance premium of any kind, or registered to vote, etc., etc., etc.? My point is that it seems to me that the mature, responsible, contributing citizens caught up in this time of need are actually being penalized for the responsible actions they have taken in living their lives. If we happened to have personal insurance policies, which is the responsible way that most of us have been taught to practice all of our lives, then we are being denied any further financial assistance from the very programs set up by our government to help us! This just does not make sense to me. It actually encourages many of us to consider being irresponsible and to just give up on taking care of ourselves, I think.

My government has shown me that they do not care about those of us who have struggled so hard to take care of ourselves and contribute to making America strong and proud. In my time of need, I feel forgotten and punished by my government for working hard all my life and being a responsible citizen. Just doesn't make much sense to me how they run these programs. The system encourages us to be strong and independent, but then blatantly penalizes us for it!

NUMBING THE PAIN AND ALTERING THE MOOD

I, like many other survivors, have sought counseling to help deal with the trauma of this disaster. It has been my experience throughout the counseling sessions to be offered numerous types and dosages of mind numbing and mood altering drugs. I am not against taking medications meant to heal wounds and diseases, but with a broken spirit and a traumatized mental state, I am not convinced that drugs are our answer. I think if we masks the emotional disorders created by the massive losses left by this disaster, we might be setting ourselves up for future problems in our society. I suppose that time will tell.

SHOCK AND DESPAIR

RUBBLE AND RUINS
DEATH AND DESTRUCTION
WALKING AMONG IT
MAKES YOU WONDER WHAT YOU ARE DOING

SEARCHING FOR YOUR PAST
AND YOUR DREAMS OF YOUR FUTURE
LOOKING FOR A PIECE OF WHO YOU WERE
AND WONDERING WHERE YOU WILL GO FROM HERE

AS YOU SEE EVERYTHING, EVERYTHING . . . .
EVERYTHING
LAYING DESTROYED BENEATH YOUR FEET
YOUR HEART AND SOUL CAN DO NOTHING
BUT SIMPLY, DEEPLY WEEP

NO TRACE OF THE PAST
NO HINT OF TOMORROW
WE ARE SCARED AND CONFUSED
WE ARE FILLED WITH SO MUCH SORROW

BEGINNING AGAIN ~ ~ STANDING TALL

Miles of destruction
And smiles of hope
Rescues and recoveries
And learning to cope

We struggle and we fight
To crawl back from under it all
Discovering how to stand tall again
And always praying that we won't fall

This body should have never had the strength to withstand the physical fight for life against the full force and fury of Hurricane Katrina, but it did. Explain all you will about what adrenalin can do for a body, but I choose to believe it was strength directly from God that carried me through those hours. My faith won't allow me to believe that it was any other way.

Isaiah 40:31 . . . but those who hope in the Lord will renew their strength. They will soar on wings like eagles; they will run and not grow weary, they will walk and not be faint. NIV

THE MEANING OF THE INK

For many years I have worn a tattoo on the inside of my lower right arm. Some have thought it wasn't very "lady like" and wondered why I would have my body marked that way. After the hurricane, the meaning of those markings became vividly clear in my mind, and more importantly in my heart, more so than ever before.

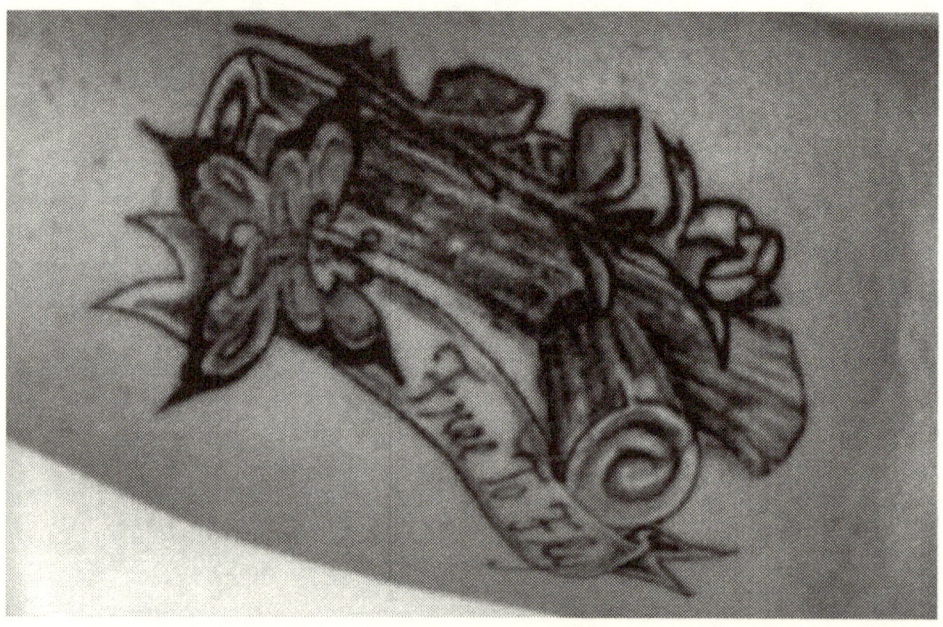

The cross represents my faith . . . . the rose is a symbol of love . . . . and the butterfly is a sign of hope.

FAITH, LOVE and HOPE ~ ~ with these three, I am set free to be all that God has intended me to be.

DESTRUCTION AND REBIRTH

On the wings of the angels
And in the palm of His hand
We rode out the hurricane
As it destroyed the land

The rage and the fury
Was evident all about
It was worse than we imagined
Truly a nightmare being acted out

The winds screamed like demons
And the waters raged and swirled
Devouring everything in its path
As though attempting to create a brand new world

PRAYERS AND DOCTRINES

I have never even pretended to understand all of our different religions. I have chosen to believe that we all have one and the same Heavenly Father ultimately, no matter what or how our many different man made doctrines are written and practiced. On that day, in the midst of my prayers, I remember asking God to hear all our prayers, no matter what religion we practiced in this world, and no matter whom each one of us might be praying to that day. I know there were an awful lot of "Hail Mary's" going up from that bush that so many of my coworkers clung to, but as for me, I was talking directly to God. At that moment in time, no amount of wind, tornadoes, flying debris or raging waters could interfere with my direct line to God. He heard my prayers and my cries for help in spite of all the chaos and confusion of the hurricane. The power lines came down around us, and all known forms of man made communications failed, but my open and direct line with my God never faultered . . . . it never failed. He was there and He heard my prayers. He carried me safely through the worst disaster man has ever known in this United States, and I thank Him every day for still being very alive and in charge of His world and our lives. I realize that we each have choices about how we live our lives and what we choose to believe. As for me, I am so thankful that I know my God and that He knows me. I know that He still lives today and never turns away from us no matter what our circumstances might be.

REST AND REASSURANCE

I won't know for awhile if I will be awarded worker's compensation insurance or social security disability, but rather I receive either or not, all will be okay. It was okay BEFORE August 29, 2005. It was miraculously okay ON August 29, 2005, and it WILL BE okay each and every day from now until my time in this world is done. My faith makes me believe that, and His word says it.

Romans 8:28 . . . . . . And we know that all things work together for good to them that love God, to them who are the called according to His purpose. KJV

DARKNESS ~ ALL ACROSS THE LAND AND DEEP IN MY SOUL

As night fell over the Bay on that Monday evening of the hurricane, I shuddered. It was so dark and still outside. There was no movement it seemed . . . . no signs of life to me. The only sounds I could hear piercing through the silence were the deep, gut wrenching screams inside of me. Though I was quiet and in shock on the outside, I knew I was screaming and crying on the inside. I felt lost. I felt frightened. I felt abandoned. I was scared for the very first time I could remember in years. I wanted to be anywhere but there, and I was sure that no one even knew we were there. I felt as though we had been cut off from the rest of the world and would surely never find our way back. Somehow I instinctively knew of the shock and horror that others must be feeling as they saw the pictures and heard the reports of the devastation. It was so very, very dark now, and I felt so very alone. I remember hearing my son describe to me how he felt while watching it all unfold from Las Vegas, NV. He said that during the time frame that the hurricane hovered over the coast line and up until they finally heard from me the next day, everything had just turned totally dark for him. He knew the trouble I was in as I fought to survive, and he felt the struggle it was for me to stay alive. I've heard stories all my life of how love connects us in ways much deeper than the heart, and I know for sure now that my son and I are connected through our souls.

I could feel myself shaking and weeping inside for my own Mother that night as I sat waiting in that quiet, dark stillness. The panic inside of me was like a frightened child when they think they are lost. I still, to this day, feel that same panicked feeling deep inside from time to time, and I've always slept with a light on since that first dark and lonely night.

RESPECTFUL SILENCE

I feel as though it is disrespectful to speak of so many of the things I saw that day and in the first few days that followed. Those of us who were left alive were almost in a zombie state of shock, and we knew we were the lucky ones. I pray always that those who were taken that day were allowed to pass from this world in a peaceful way. I envision those who were taken by the sea to be happy and content to rummage through our buried treasures there with them that we can no longer see. I've always been better if I could see a picture of things that I can't quite understand, so imagining this vision in some small way helps my own healing proceed.

THE ANSWERED CALL

You know, I have read a lot of the articles about what went wrong prior to and immediately following this disaster, but there is something you all need to know. On that morning . . . . August 29, 2005 . . . . an emergency call went out from an inside dispatch line at Waveland PD and I heard God answer that line and instantly respond. For all that did go wrong that day, and continues to go wrong even today . . . . when God answered our call that morning, everything went right.

"FLOATER'S FUND"

For all of the donations that have poured into Waveland Police Department since that day, monetary and otherwise, I have yet to see a dime of it. Not even a phone call from the Mayor or the Chief to ask if I am okay or if I need anything to help me find my way back to living a normal life. I often wonder what those who donated might say if they really knew. What comes to mind for me is that beach bum's phrase set to music that says something along the lines of how much money he has made only to find that he's pissed it all away. Where are all the funds intended to help those of us who were there that day? I've been told that they are randomly passing it out at their own discretion, and certainly in no fair and equal way. Someone who was not even with us that day as we fought to stay alive supposedly has it all in a bank somewhere and has labeled it in a joking sort of way as "the floater's fund". Makes me laugh sarcastically when I think about how I might see that money has been spent someday. If I live long enough to drive that Beach Boulevard in Waveland, MS once it's rebuilt, I believe I will recognize many of the names on the million dollar mansion mailboxes all along the way!

To quote a truth I once read and have never forgotten:

"A crooked peace officer is just a damned abomination, that's all you can say about it. He's ten times worse than the criminal."

THE GAME

The mission of the police department has always been to protect and serve. That should always begin at home, taking care of our own first and foremost. Without the safety of first responders as their priority, how could our city officials ever expect to carry out our mission? They made a terrible mistake by not upholding their responsibility to protect us, their city employees, and it has cost a great many of us a great deal. As a dispatcher, I no longer feel confident in believing that my Chief and Mayor will provide and follow through with a plan to assure my safety in the time of an emergency. If I cannot be assured of my own safety and protection, how can I confidently assure someone else in their time of need during an emergency? The trauma of the experience that I faced with Waveland PD on the morning that Hurricane Katrina made landfall has left me unable to perform the duties required of an emergency dispatcher. I have been left with a feeling of helplessness, both for myself and for others. I feel alone, abandoned and helpless as a result of the trauma. City officials chose to play Russian roulette with my life that day . . . . I am so glad God intervened on my behalf that day and He won the game in spite of their bad calls.

FINDING MY WAY BACK

Readjusting to life after Hurricane Katrina is tough. It is hard to face each day and other people who have no way of understanding how all of this has changed me. I am struggling each and every day to get back to being the woman that I used to be.

How am I going to do that? I pray and wait patiently everyday for my answers.

"So do not fear, for I am with you; do not be dismayed, for I am your God. I will strengthen you and help you; I will uphold you with my righteous right hand."

Isaiah 41:10 NIV

ALONG THE JOURNEY

Life is a journey
That we travel day by day
Some things that we collect, we keep
Other things, we give away

It's not the tangible gifts
That we should hold so dear
It's the love of each other
That we should always keep near

When our time is over . . .
The time we leave this life
We should leave our gifts with others
In their hearts . . . forever to hold tight

It might be a smile
Perhaps a kind word or two
The everlasting, irreplaceable gifts
Those, I pray, I will leave with you

POSITIVE PROGRESS

In the year that has come and gone since that horrifying day, I have made positive progress in so many ways. I have been able to settle in a nice area far away from the rubble and ruins, and I have been blessed to have my daughter by my side every step of the way. We were taken under the wings of numerous angels, some of whom we have yet to meet face to face. They poured out their love on us in many, many ways in the first few months after the hurricane. We were offered food and shelter, clothing and shoes, car repairs and even cash to help us along the way. I remember them all in my prayers every day, and I feel that they each still do the same for us. I have tried in good faith and actions to continue life as though nothing ever happened, but that has proven to be impossible. I suffer panic attacks now when faced with the responsibilities and requirements of being a police dispatcher, and I have even noticed a claustrophobic feeling just being confined behind those locked doors now. I am undergoing counseling to help work through all the fears I have now and will always hope to be able to return to that field of work. I have filled some of my days during this past year by working part time in a woman's clothing store. God opened that door for me when I least expected it, and I will always be thankful for the lady friends He introduced me to there. It is a store that I have shopped in for years, and the perks I receive as an employee has made it affordable for me to restock the wardrobe that I lost to the storm. God works in such wonderful, mysterious ways because although I am not a customer service sort of gal, I do love clothes!

I still have not quite been able to find my way back into the mainstream of life yet, but I figure after experiencing what I did in that hurricane, it will be alright if I just sit down beside the quiet, still waters and prayerfully watch the world go by for awhile.

And he withdrew himself into the wilderness, and prayed.
Luke 5:16 KJV

SNAKES, ANTS AND PSALMS

I had almost forgotten about the snakes! They were plentiful and visible all around us in the water. I remember seeing one trailing directly behind one of the other dispatchers as she was being helped to the edge of the roof of the building. I shudder even now as I think of it. Water moccasins, I believe they were. Also in the Gulf waters that day were sea turtles and fish and frogs. I believe I saw a lot of jelly fish there too, milky pink and emitting a sort of glow. What I remember most though were the ants. They were everywhere . . . even in my hair. My body still bears the scars even today from the biting and stinging from the ants. There was no way to keep them away, and even when I felt the fire from their bite, I couldn't let go to brush them off for fear of being swept away by the powerful pull of the waters. We were truly trapped there in the full fury and chaos of the raging tidal wave. I remember pleading silently inside "God, please oh please won't you get us out of this alive?" I know the prayer and promises of Psalms 23, but for the life of me, I could not get those words to form in my mind, much less come out of my mouth at that time. I was struggling and afraid and fighting to keep my head above the water, and it was only later as I lay stretched full out and face down on that hard, cold tin roof that the words of that chapter in Psalms came pouring out of me. Over and over and over again, from the very depths of my soul, they repeated themselves voluntarily, louder and louder until the real, true meaning of every word finally, finally took hold. When I surrendered my fear totally to God, and I could feel the muscles in my body beginning to relax, then it all began to come back to me. Every bible verse, every Sunday school nursery rhyme, every promise I had ever read from God's great word became the strength I needed to continue to hang on. Those words wrapped me in warmth like a blanket and comforted my soul. We are instructed to store up His word in our hearts, and now I know why.

AND THE GREATEST IS LOVE

The most important lesson from this disaster that I want others to understand is the need to teach our children and help them understand the real meaning of God's great commandment to love one another. I believe that is our sole purpose for time here on Earth, and it was during some of the darkest hours of my life after the hurricane that I understood God's full meaning of that commandment to us. We must, without hesitation or too much forethought, reach out to others in gestures of love. When one hand reaches out to touch one heart, the good that can come from it is beyond measure. It doesn't take an army, or FEMA, or even a state governor to change the state our world is in. It takes one friend, or a family unit, or even an entire community to take the hand of just one person standing closest to them, and sincerely saying and meaning "I understand your concerns and I am willing to help all that I can." I think what God knew about loving one another that maybe far too many of us still do not understand, is that loving each other isn't hard, and it doesn't have to cost us anything. God's love simply happens when we reach out to each other with eye contact, a smile or a touch of the hand, and do it with a sincere, honest and pure heart. We just need each other in this world, in the good times and the bad. No man is an island. We all need a friend.

The outpouring of aid and love and compassion to those on the coast has been unbelievably generous. My faith in mankind and our purpose here on Earth has not only been restored, but multiplied and expanded tremendously. Our brothers and sisters, from every neighborhood and all walks of life, rose up and moved forward toward the direst conditions left by this storm along the Southern coastal areas of these United States. They met our needs, one on one, without hesitation or rules and regulations. Even before our President did his first flyover to view the complete devastation, our neighbors were there beside us holding our hands and our hearts. I am ashamed of our government's response, but I am still so very, very proud to be an American. Had this experience happened to me in any other country of this world, I wonder if I would have survived it at all.

MY NEIGHBOR ~ MY FRIEND

I have walked among the ruins and I have breathed the stench of death
I have witnessed pain and weeping and I have suffered like all the rest

We lost our worldly possessions and many lost loved ones too
We were numb, lifeless and afraid, and while we searched for answers
There was you.

All different colors and sizes and shapes . . . One helping another
One at a time . . . . one by one.
You helping just one other is all it really takes.

We thought you would look like our uncle . . . the one in the white
house on the hill. We expected to see our military with all of our troops
coming through, but when we looked around, the one we saw was you.

My neighbor, my butcher, my banker . . . . my friend
Each time we looked up, we saw you again.
You didn't have papers and forms with all that "red tape"
You helping just one other is all it really takes.

I thank you my neighbor, my butcher, my banker and my friend
It is because of your helping hand
That I have been able to begin to live again.

The grant money and gifts that are tied up in "red tape"
Still seem useless and out of reach to date
Thank you again . . . my neighbor, my butcher, my banker . . . . my friend
You helping just one other is all it really takes.

GRANTS AND PRIVATE DONATIONS

Our government chain of command, all the way from the white house on the hill to the state capital leaders, then right on down to the county seats and local city leaders . . . . what a joke. The rich get richer and the honest, hard working folks just keep doing what we have always done. We persevere. We pray and we survive. We reach deep inside ourselves and pull out that spirit of neighborly love and we share it. Waiting on a handout from our government is like believing in a fairy tale. We dream it and we may even feel it, but we very rarely, if ever, see it.

When you give in the face of need, look them in the eyes and make sure the one who needs it gets the help. Otherwise, we can never be really sure of where it goes.

SOCIAL STATUS

I thank you Katrina, for breaking down all social lines and bringing us all eye to eye. The doctors and lawyers, and yes, even the police chiefs all became equal in life with that one single wave that crashed ashore and wiped everything away. Peering into each others eyes in the hours immediately following the storm, the shock was visible and we could see deep into each others weeping souls. It did not matter what we had acquired before that day. It was all gone now. It had all been washed away. Our hunger and our fear were equal for all of us in that moment in time. Money didn't matter because there was nothing left to buy, and status didn't mean a thing as we all stood knee deep in the rubble and ruins . . . . for that time, we all stood eye to eye. For as lost as we all felt, I think in that instant we all found something in each other that I believe we should not let die. Our basic needs are all the same as humans, no matter how high up that social ladder we might choose to climb. Do not judge one another is certainly another one of the many lessons I learned that day.

STRAIGHT AND NARROW

I don't profess my Christian walk to be any more straight and narrow than any others. In fact, I have been known more times than not, to take the side road off the beaten path. I am sure many have thought I was most certainly lost in my life from time to time, but I always knew I was never alone. In the bottom of the valley, face down in the mud, He was there beside me. Always and patiently remaining by my side and encouraging me to pick my head up and simply breathe. The breath of life that He has shared with me so many, many times has given me the courage and strength to continue to struggle to survive. He hears my prayers and provides my needs. Without the faith of believing the things that I cannot yet see, I would have given up long ago.

TOUGH CHOICES

As far as my decision to file for worker's compensation and social security benefits, I struggle with that decision even today. I did not anticipate such a long, slow recovery. I did not know that the trauma and fear of what I went through that day had scarred me so deeply. I never expected to need any assistance to regain my confidence and strength to stand on my own again. My independence has been threatened, and my fight to get it back has taken me through a system that I have discovered needs to be looked at. When a responsible, hard working American citizen is judged and made to fight legally for the financial support from funds that are rightfully his, something is very, very wrong with our American system. We give our lives to the betterment of our country, and our efforts are shunned in our time of need. I wish I had been keeping every dollar that I have ever paid into my government's social security plan, and every penny of matched funds on my state retirement plan buried somewhere in a coffee can! It would have proven to be more accessible and useful for me that way than entrusting it to the "powers that be" has proven to be.

CHAOS, CONFUSION AND CHARITIES

Many, many businesses donated huge amounts of merchandise and services to help the hurricane victims, but those donations proved to be inaccessible to most of us. The donations and offers of charitable services were channeled mainly through our top two American charity organizations, and neither organization was aware of, or would acknowledge availability of donated services when I inquired about them. The representatives of these charities never even offered to find out about the donations for me. They were more concerned about rather or not I had already received help of any kind from their group, and they both treated me as though I were trying to get more than my share of help. I was frustrated and aggravated, and so very disappointed in how these charities operate. I feel quite sure that no where near all of the contributions made toward our recovery were ever given to those of us in need.

THE GOLDEN RULE

A state congressman was one of the first outside officials that I recall seeing on the ground with those of us who had actually been there when Katrina came ashore. It might have even been as early as that Monday evening, but I can't be sure of that. What I do know for sure though is that he was genuinely concerned for us all, and he was right there in the mud and the blood and the tears with us all. Our own Mayor wasn't even as much there with us as our congressman. The city mayor was in a deeper state of shock than even the rest of us appeared to be it seemed. He would not look any of us in the eye and he never took the time to speak, not even to ask how we were or to say thank you for staying to protect our city. I felt he owed us that much . . . a thank you for staying, and an apology for requiring us to stay. It not only would have been nice to have him speak, but also certainly would have made the next few days there a little easier for me. He didn't speak at all and I will always wonder why. I don't recall seeing my Chief at all over those next few days. I know he was there with us on the day of the storm, and I know he survived by holding on to that bush with so many of the others, but I don't know what happened to him after that. I left the coast on Thursday after the hurricane came in on Monday, and I have only heard from him once since then. Over a year has passed now and he still has not taken the time to find out how I am. I risked my life to help him during the hurricane, but it does not seem to have meant anything to him. A simple "Thank you" and "I'm sorry" would have made this past year so much easier for me. I hope he knows the Golden Rule, and I hope those words will be etched at the entrance of every city building that is rebuilt in Waveland, MS.

Do for other people whatever you would like to have them do for you.
This is what the Jewish Law and the early preachers said.
Matthew 7:12 NLV

RISING UP TO REBUILD

Look above the devastation
Amidst all the hurt and pain
Along with all our losses
What could we have possibly gained?

A deeper understanding
A greater love and respect
For all that came before us
For all that hasn't come yet

As we rise up from the ruins
While we rebuild our future land
Let's keep generations to come in mind
Give them reasons to cherish and understand

There is a need to nurture
And rebuild some memories from our past
To look into their futures
And give them the best of what we had

Our visions for today
Will far outlast us all
Make sure we are thinking of others
When we make that final call

LEARNING TO FLY

I remember the story my son told me of how he, and many of the crew from the theater where he worked, watched the weather channel from Las Vegas as Hurricane Katrina made her trek across the Gulf of Mexico. He was working an evening job, and each night when the show closed, they would all gather at a local watering hole and party until daylight. That Sunday night, August 28, 2005, was the same as many others before, except for Hurricane Katrina. They all knew that "Ben's Mom" was working on the coast, and that kept them glancing at the television in the bar all night. They drank and laughed and swapped storm stories until around 6am Vegas time when they watched the hurricane cross over land near Buras, LA. They breathed a sigh of relief and lifted their glasses to toast, thinking at that moment that I was spared another close call and would be safe. My son said that before they had time to sit their glasses back down, they watched the storm take a turn . . . . and fear gripped him deep and hard. The laughter stopped, the group got quiet and the drinks stopped flowing. They watched in horror as Hurricane Katrina made her way in a Northeasterly direction straight toward Waveland, MS. He said that in that moment, nausea overtook him and he felt weak and sick. As their eyes remained glued to the television screen, and silence surrounded them all, reality was evident that Ben's Mom wasn't safe after all. He said that the mood was so very somber and the silence was deafening and awkward, so he decided to speak to ease the worry and tension. What he said in that moment made them all laugh and will be remembered and repeated in our family for years to come each time my story is retold. His comment was "Oh Lord, the roads between Bay St. Louis and Jackson, MS are gonna' be paved with Oprah magazines because my Mom is a charter subscriber and she has every Oprah magazine that has ever been printed!" He said he knew that our house would be gone, and could only pray that I was already gone from the PD and would somehow be okay. As they left that bar at daybreak, he said his world got very, very dark. He said he knew. He said that he could feel deep inside that his Mother was in trouble and fighting to survive. I have heard that people who are close in heart really can feel each others emotions and experiences. It's true. My son's heart broke and wept, and his spirit was quiet and dark until he finally knew for sure about me. When he heard that I had called and that I was okay, that's when he felt the light come back on deep inside of himself. Love . . . . what an amazing, wonderful, God given mystery! The body can be described and studied just like a machine, but our emotions . . . they are a gift from our Heavenly Father.

Something that I heard once seems fitting to share here . . . . ***When we come to the edge of the light we know, and are about to step off into the darkness of the unknown, of this we can be sure . . . . . . either God will provide something solid to stand on or . . . we will be taught to fly.***

This painting was the result of my son's fear and anguish in response to Hurricane Katrina's fury. It was his therapy as a means to his healing.

TIES THAT BIND

Throughout this past year, my daughter has been such a source of strength to me. For that, I will forever see her in a different light. We are both very strong, vibrant, powerful women and have deep rooted strengths inside of us. While my internal strength wavered over this past year, hers flourished and sprouted more roots. Our family tree is stronger and more secure than it was before the disaster. The only difference in the way we have viewed this life changing event has been because of the 29 year difference in our ages. At 23 years old, she was sad to have lost all of her worldly belongings, but so thankful that we were alive. I, on the other hand, have wept for my lost past . . . . prayed for my uncertain future . . . . and rejoiced with her that He held me in His hands and allowed me to survive. Each new day truly is a gift from God.

NOSTALGIA

A lifetime of treasures are gone with the wind
The memories remain nurtured deep within.

I browse the shelves of new items, each one shiny and bright
I long for the old, familiar . . . those things that seemed to fit me just
right.

Open my heart Lord, so that I might truly see
All that YOU have in store for me.

I will cherish the memories as I start all new
Watching and waiting for direction from you.

When I pass the old and familiar I will smile softly and whisper Thank
You
For I know that with time and nurturing, all these new things will
become old and familiar too.

BLESSINGS

My daughter and I were blessed with the support of prayers and financial gifts from two church groups in upstate New York, as well as many family members and friends. Their concern and generosity helped us to be able to purchase the basic necessities for setting up household again. I still to this day have not met many of those who reached out to us personally, but I know them all in my heart. They are my brothers and sisters in Christ and were my neighbors in our time of need. They shared God's love in the most tangible ways that helped to restore my stability and my dignity. To be so in need, and yet to have nothing to give in return for their gifts, surely taught me the true meaning of loving one another. They loved us enough to share in our time of need, and I was taught how to love others enough to simply be willing and grateful in accepting what God had called them to do. The joy they expressed in their giving caused my own heart to overflow with their kindness and love.

God will provide in our lives whatever we need if we are just humble enough to receive it. Hurricane Katrina tore down my fortress of independence and humbled me. I thank God for the lesson from the blessings in the midst of the storm.

MAMA ~ MORE THAN JUST A NAME

One very sweet, comforting memory I have from the long, lonesome days and nights immediately following the hurricane stems from a conversation with my night sergeant. As we waited for outside help to arrive in the days following the disaster, there were opportunities for us to share things with each other that otherwise might never had been said. For all the years that I had worked with this man, he had always called me "Mama" for as long as I could remember and I never really understood why. Some days it would sound like a loving compliment, but other times I could hear a tone in his voice that didn't seem so nice. On that Monday night, in the quiet stillness of the chaos, he came to me to talk for awhile. He sat beside me and held my hand, and he let me cry for a while. He whispered softly as he hugged me and said "It's alright Mama. We all made it out alive." He continued to talk kindly and sincerely and this is what he said . . . . "I know you have always wondered why I call you Mama, so let me see if I can help you understand. It's because Mama is the first woman that a man ever loves, and she is the last woman that he wants to see before he dies. It is out of complete love and respect for you that I call you Mama. I know that you were worried about all of us worrying about you out there in the storm, but you weren't a burden for us at all out there. You thought I was holding you Mama, but the real truth is that you were holding me. I couldn't let you go Mama . . . . then I wouldn't have had anyone to hold on to. So see, I needed you out there as much as you needed me. Without each other, none of us would have made it."

Not a burden and called by the sweetest name a man has ever known . . . . I feel very lucky to have known and worked with that night sergeant.

Greater love hath no man than this, that a man lay down his life for his friends. John 15:13 KJV

GOING HOME

About a month after the hurricane, while I was in Las Vegas at my son's house, I got a call from the Chief. He ask me to come back to live and work in Waveland. I remember the feeling of hope and exhilaration that I felt. I packed up the few things that had been donated to me and the things I had purchased over that past month, and I loaded it all in my daughter's little Ford Escort. The total combination of all that she and I now owned in life fit in the back seat and trunk of her little car! It was all that we had, but we held on to it proudly and started the 1800 mile trip back home to the coast. Three nights and four days later, we arrived. It was a Friday afternoon and in spite of the devastation of the entire area, I was happy to be there. Our first stop was the address where the police department had previously been. What I found there offended me. The highway out front, and the entire parking lot, was crowded with 18 wheeler box trailers full of supplies. They were locked up tight and being guarded and monitored by the police officers. There were plastic containers lined up around the parking lot with the names of officers and dispatchers written on them with black marker. There was a shade tent erected in front of the building and a state park ranger and a reserve police officer were cooking something on an outdoor grill underneath it. There were ice chests full of bottled water, fruit juice and sodas all around. I saw one single wide office trailer and one camper trailer parked on the side of the lot. I looked for the Chief but he was nowhere around. I found his wife in the single wide office trailer, and it was evident to me from the first word she spoke that she had taken charge of the police department and was controlling everything and everyone on the grounds. She advised me that there were no more trailers available for my daughter and I to live in, but that we were welcome to stay in her daughter's trailer. We were given sets of keys for a couple of other trailers parked out at Buccaneer State Park and told to look at them and decide if we wanted to live in one of them. They were vacant, but only because none had generator hookups, and the park facilities for supplying these utilities to those parking spaces, had been washed away by the hurricane. We were forced to stay that Friday night and the next few nights in the Chief's daughter's trailer. The campsite where the trailers were parked is right on Beach Blvd. on the West end of the city, and that area is notorious for flooding completely each time the tide comes in! Mud was still knee deep in that area, and the stench of dead bodies was everywhere. All recognizable landmarks in the city had been destroyed, and it was hard to find our way around when driving anywhere in the area. I felt lost. I felt ship wrecked on a mangled, torn, destroyed island out in the middle of nowhere. When the sun came up and warmed the Earth, the stench of mold and mildew and death was everywhere, and so thick and heavy in the air that I could hardly breathe. At night there was no light at all and the total darkness and sounds of the night were frightening to me. I am a grown woman, very strong in character and determination, but all of this was far too much for me to take in. I was scared and lost and felt as frightened about my current situation and my future as I had ever felt in my adult life. I had my 23 year old daughter there with me, and I knew I could not stay there in those living conditions if for no other reason than for her. It was dangerous, it was lonely and we were totally surrounded by death and devastation even now, four weeks after the disaster. The dispatch center for the city had been combined with other agencies and was now located many miles away from the coast, in a double wide trailer way up in the country. I had no vehicle to get back and forth there since the hurricane had destroyed both of my personal vehicles, so even if I stayed I couldn't get back and forth to work. I wasn't sure I could even dispatch again after the memory of those last phone calls at the PD, and then the trauma that we faced for those six or seven hours that Hurricane Katrina hung over the coast. I wasn't really sure of much of anything that weekend that I returned to Waveland, other than realizing that life had changed totally there and I knew for sure that nothing was ever going to put it back to the way it used to be again. I was sad. I was lonely and afraid. On the following Monday morning, as I watched the sun coming up over Coleman Bay, I got my daughter and I back into that little Ford Escort and we drove away. I knew for sure that day that God did not bring me through the storm and spare my life for me to crawl back down there in the middle of all of the remaining death and destruction to wither away. There was no life left there on the coast, but just 20 miles up the highway north of there, there was. So on that Monday morning, my daughter and I packed ourselves back into that little Ford Escort and we drove away. I cried as we left, and I still to this day cry each and every time I return.

TEARS

It was almost four full months after the hurricane before I felt myself begin to crack and crumble and come unglued. My insides felt like a fine piece of china that had been shattered into so many, many tiny pieces that the pieces resembled powdery dust as they began to separate from my soul and fall apart. God only knows what had held me together up until that day, but I think it was the sheer shock of it all. I had carried myself away from that coast and out of the ruins without even being aware of the movements my body was making. I was unaware of any feelings inside of myself. I only remember being so very, very thankful that I had come out of it alive. On that day when I began to feel my insides starting to stir, it was a tear that surfaced first. I remember feeling it roll down my cheek, and I watched it hit the floor. Uncontrollably, and without being able to stop them, that one tear was followed by many, many more. For two days and nights I wept from deep inside. I remember the feeling of exhaustion and wishing not to cry. It was December 23, 2005 when I met with a counselor and I was sure by that time that I was losing my mind. I don't know if I even spoke that day with him in his office, but I know that I cried. Everything . . . all of it . . . life as I had known it, had been swept away and left no traces of my past, not even deep inside of me on this particular day. I went to him totally shattered and broken and aimlessly wandering and lost. I must have frightened even him to a certain degree because he scheduled another appointment to see me again in just another week. He understood my fragile state, I think. He recognized that the state of shock that had been holding me together up to that point was wearing thin, and he was there with me to witness my very first steps of recovery beginning. I've continued with the counseling even to this day, and I have even been introduced to some prescription drugs to help me along the way. One is for my nerves to keep them calm and still. Another is for my jumbled mind to help me think straight and figure out what is real. Then there is a third one that is meant to help me sleep, but even with the medication some days I still weep. I am not convinced that the drugs they offered for my bruised spirit and empty mental state were totally for me. I stopped taking them early on and decided to just face my demons as they come.

What I lost that day of the hurricane true enough was only stuff, but it was the lifetime I had built in my 52 years on this Earth, and so very much of it defined who I was. I walked away from there three days after that storm feeling broken and empty and numb. It was that day in December, when I felt the first tear fall, that I knew a new life for me had begun. Change isn't easy, but it is inevitable and we can either embrace it or choose to reject it. It is with open arms and a willing heart, as well as a bruised, but not broken spirit that I can face tomorrow. *Because He lives, I can face tomorrow . . . because He lives, all fear is gone.* When I weep, and I still do even today, I feel the tears cleansing my soul and awakening my spirit to the possibilities of what might come next in my life. My empty vase is half full again and I can see it overflowing with beautiful yellow roses, the symbol of the joys of love and life and fellowship with good friends. My life is not over, oh contraire, for each day is a new beginning and we can each choose to begin again from there.

GRIEVING

Experts say the grievance period can take up to three years. It took me seven years to get through the loss of my best friend when my marriage broke up, and I still grieve for my family unit all the time. I am 53 years old now, and I wonder if God has it in His plans for my life to exist long enough to get completely through this grievance period. There is an expression that says "those things that do not kill us make us stronger." I have become a pillar of strength through the years. I have lots of proverbial scars covering life's wounds, and scar tissue is a lot stronger and thicker than our original skin. I have scars which would lead others to believe that my wounds have healed, but underneath they still bleed most days. Other times I just feel numb under the thickness of the scars. But deep inside . . . . underneath it all, there is still much joy dancing around inside of me and that joy is what still makes life worthwhile.

EVERYTHING WE NEED

A Nomad . . . . A Gypsy
A Roustabout . . . . A Rolling Stone
Wherever I wander
I will always be home

Carrying no baggage
And free to drift around
Discovering and uncovering
Treasures to be found

When I long for the comforts
Of home and hearth
I will be still and be quiet
And I will find it all in my heart

Everything we need
Is buried deep inside
For it's only when you lose it all
That you are truly free to fly

SHE IS A SURVIVOR

For all of you I left behind . . . I carry you in my heart and I know that Bay Saint Louis/Waveland did not die in Katrina. I see her clearly—I hear her sweet sounds, and I smell the salt water. Each and every time I close my eyes and let my mind wander . . . I am there again, just the way it was and will always be to those of us who loved her so. I can still—I will always and forever, hear the gentle waves and the soft distant squawking of the seagulls. I close my eyes and I can feel the warm sand between my toes and the sea foam lapping at my ankles. She will never die, for she is a survivor just like you and I.

SIX MONTHS HAS COME AND GONE

03/13/06—I went to the coast today. Curiosity and lonesomeness won out and I could no longer stay away. I have missed that place every day. The drive down seemed long . . . . it seemed so very far from North Mississippi. I went to the police department first and it seemed cold and empty there. They were putting on such a professional face and trying so hard to still be in charge, yet there is nothing left there to be in charge of! It is all gone now. Six and a half months after that hurricane and still not enough has come back to that area to make a difference there. There are lots of people and cars and FEMA trailers everywhere, but still no life there. It feels empty and dead and sad there still. The destruction and litter and debris are all still so very evident everywhere you look . . . . and the stench! Lord, the smell down there almost took my breath away. Sewer and rotting death hangs heavy over the entire area, and even the midday rain shower stunk like rotten seafood and raw sewage! The knats and termites are everywhere and so visible that they made my skin crawl and itch long after we had left the area. Driving up the beachfront, from Highway 49 in Gulfport to Biloxi, is still unrecognizable to both my daughter and I. We could see very few buildings or structures of any sort that we could identify. Looking out into the Gulf we could still see the remnants of trees and debris so thick in the water—and things, remnants and remains of peoples lives are washed up everywhere. I wonder how many folks still go there every day . . . standing and watching and waiting . . . praying to maybe see a piece of their lives washed up there one day. Sad and empty and lonely and dead . . . . that's what I saw there today.

My daughter still walks the property of the lot where the remains of our lives still lay. The house is still there, crumbled and broken and rotting away. What the weather and the looters haven't taken, the termites are eating away. She recognized lots of things today. Her laptop computer, her mattress and part of the bed frame, and a wicker bookshelf that was in her bedroom with the books still stacked on it just as they were that fateful day! Amazing what we see, and unbelievable to remember all the things we once had that we can no longer see. Today she endured the knats and the rain long enough to come away with a broken, splintered piece of wood from one of our kitchen chairs, and a string of muddy, faded plastic Mardi Gras beads bearing a shiny, red crawfish that we once so proudly displayed. Somehow, maybe these few trinkets and pieces of the life we once knew there will help her heal and move forward from this tragedy. Maybe she will see the real values in life . . . . and also in memories. To remember where we came from might somehow make going forward into the unknown future just a little easier and less fearful for both of us. I certainly hope so. My faith takes the fear away, but it doesn't make it any easier as far as not knowing for sure about things from day to day.

I remembered today how many, many times I stood at my kitchen window looking out across the backyard to a junky, little blue house there just over the fence. I sat on my back porch swing many a day and fussed about the loud talking, rap music and busy traffic in and out over there around that little blue house. There was always a crowd around there it seemed, laughing and cooking out on the grill, working on cars or cleaning up the yard and burning bonfires with the scraps from the trash and the trees. I cursed them under my breath many a time for the noise and the smoke and the loud, bumping rap music. I found out today that they all died in that little, old, and junky looking blue house. My heart broke a little deeper than it already is, and my soul wept again deep, deep inside. They didn't deserve to die. It must have been so terrifying for them all that day—when the wind and the waters just came rushing in and washed it all away. And the sand it brought inland, then leaving several feet of that thick, gooey, black mud covering over top of everything as it sucked back out into the sea. It carried with it so, so much . . . people and places and things. Nine of them Lord . . . nine of them were all together in that little blue house that day. Somehow I hope they didn't know what was really happening and were gone with the first wave of the tidal surge. I don't want to think that they may have had to struggle, fighting to reach the attic first, and then their rooftop, only to be overtaken and swept away. I know that struggle and fight because I was there that day. I know the fear and the struggle and the fight for life because I came so very, very close to losing that battle that day and simply getting swept away. I do not understand why them and so many, many others that day, and not me. I do not understand, but I am so very thankful and grateful that somehow I survived that fight, and I continue to pray for those who did not. I sing praises everyday that I did.

I saw my friend Melinda today. It brought tears to my eyes when I looked at her and listened to the words she had to say. She sounds empty now . . . and full of fear all at the same time. She is consumed with confusion and uncertainty about everything it seems. Her eyes are mostly empty and grey now, with just a trace of fear and sadness left deep inside her somewhere, and her complexion and body are showing the definite signs of breaking down under the stress and strain of it all. Trying to rebuild and go on with life just as though this event was just another little stumbling block along life's way is hard enough, but then waking up to and walking around in it, and then going to sleep again in the middle of all that rubble and ruin and stench everyday is truly paying a tole on her. Mentally and physically she has become one of the "walking dead" there among many others. They continue to function and they try to smile, but the life has pretty much left most of those I saw who still remain there. It's different for the volunteers who just come and go there. They come full of life, are shocked by what they see and offer what little help they can, and then they leave again. I truly believe the volunteers gain something to add to their own lives just by being there. But for those who lived there before and remain there today, they exist and go through the motions from day to day, but life . . . real life . . . has simply been washed away. I pray for them all everyday and I wish they too could find what it takes to simply walk away. I know they won't . . . many can't. They will simply stay.

We saw flowers on the coast today! The azaleas are sporadically blooming. There are shades of pink and purple dotting the coastline, springing forth among the brittle, dead, brown vegetation that still covers most of the land areas. We noticed another flower there today. Bright, white flower blossoms are growing thick on some unfamiliar green vines. The white flowers are fully opened wide and almost straining to pull upward, as though trying to reach the sky. It was a strange, eerie site that made both my daughter and I uncomfortable. These were a different kind of flowers than either of us had ever seen, and I immediately had the feeling that they were poisonous. I felt like they were a fake front covering up something mysterious and evil. It felt to me as though death had come back over that area, laughing and flaunting its victory over our lives by disguising itself as something as beautiful as a flower. Almost as though the darkness of death and destruction had come back to haunt us, masking itself as pure and lily white as those flowers appeared to be.

We also went to the Dizzi Dames shop again today. We had first visited them around Christmas time. They were moving into a new building that day, after their previous location had been lost to the hurricane. Both of the ladies were there that day in December, and they were both full of hope and excitement at the thought of running their business again. This time in their shop felt very different to me. Only one owner was there and she seemed heavy with worry and looked physically exhausted to me. Her eyes had lost their twinkle and her voice was soft and weary. She appeared to be tired and I got the distinct feeling that it was a very deep, painful tired . . . like life is too tough and the days are hard to bare. She was so very nice to us, but in a very distant sort of way. I asked to use the restroom there and she led me through a maze in the house, apologizing each step of the way for the condition of the house and the mess they were in. We went from the front shop room, around through a dining room area and then into the kitchen. There in the kitchen wall was a hole cut out of the sheetrock. It was only about three feet high and maybe four feet wide. We had to stoop down and crawl through the hole into another room, and then make our way carefully around the holes in the broken floor boards and on into the bathroom. For me, it was scary and sad, shameful almost, to see these ladies holding on and trying so desperately to make a go of it all under these conditions. They are determined . . . they are desperate, but as surely as I could see it, they are tired. Life is not easy there on the coast now, but there are those who are still so determined to stay that they will crawl through the sheetrock and risk falling through the floor just to try to make it through another day. I feel sad for them. My heart breaks for them. I pray sincerely for them every day. These women managed to find a way to smile a little and share their humor with others . . . . they now have a banner displayed in the front yard that states simply and proudly: FROM HIGH CLASS TO TRAILER TRASH. Both of these Dizzi Dames are now living, or should I say existing, in FEMA camper trailers and hanging in there, just doing the best that they can day in and day out. It is hard down there on the coast for everybody now.

As we were leaving town, we noticed an old man standing on the side of the road. He held a duffle bag in one hand and a cardboard sign in the other. We didn't think of him as a panhandler, but more likely as a desperate old tired soul simply looking for a ride out of town, to anywhere else but here! He seemed too tired and weary to walk on down the road on his own, yet he looked too old and frail to stay there another day. Life is hard for everyone there on the coast these days. The easy coastal life in the paradise known as "the Bay" disappeared completely that late August 2005 day. Hurricane Katrina came in and swept it all away.

SEARCHING FOR PEACE

03/22/06: There are things that the public has seen through the media coverage during and after this disaster that do no begin to tell the real story.

Then there are those of us who were there, who really know. Try as I might to share it with you, I have scarcely touched the surface of what it was really like to have been there that day. A lot of us have stories about this disaster that need to be told. As the world forgets and moves on with life, we who were there will continue to fight to recover. We will tell and retell our stories as we remember the details of things most of us will never forget. It is our responsibility to remember and share what needs to be told, and it is also our prayer to find a way to forget it all. May those who did not survive it rest in peace, and may those of us who did survive it find the peace that we need too.

TREASURE HUNTING

03/31/06: There was such a bright sparkle in her eyes and the excitement in her voice was evident. She spoke of her four children and all that they had seen and found and picked up to take home with them from the beaches along the Gulf coast of Mississippi. Gulfport/Biloxi area specifically, but she even mentioned as far West as Bay St. Louis/Waveland, and then East as far as Ocean Springs and Woolmarket. She explained how her husband and his company had been working in the area since early on, just after Katrina passed, and now she and the four children would be permanently moving there to join him. "Oh, my children just love it there, and I plan to just hang out down there and play with my kids on the beach . . . we all just love it there!" She is searching now for a motor home to load them all up in and drive them South to their new found "land of opportunity". She spoke of how everybody down there is walking around carrying buckets and getting rich off of the quarters they are finding. The first time her children had gone to the beach, she said they found so much stuff . . . . a real silver bowie knife, clothes, toys and even a 14k gold wallet with money in it! She sounded so excited. My heart sank as I listened to her talk about it. The gold money holder had initials engraved on it and she said that although she felt a little bad about it, she let her little boy keep it anyway because he wanted it so badly. My heart sank deeper and my stomach turned . . . . I was saddened and nauseated clear down to my soul. Our lives . . . our dreams . . . our possessions are being scavenged and hunted and picked through like a big treasure hunt! I realized in that moment that some of mine and my daughter's personal belongings might be washed out to sea halfway to China and back again, or perhaps deposited on one of the little islands right out from the Mississippi coast. God forbid, please, not lying on the beaches of Biloxi somewhere, waiting to be found and carried away by strangers who think they've found a treasure that day! The quarters don't bother me so much. They came from the casinos and meant nothing to anyone in particular other than the "sharks" who owned the gambling boats. But the personal items are special, almost sacred in a sense. Should our things be touched and ciphered through, or just left to rot and wash away? Does it hurt that someone else finds our things and decides to take them home as their own? Should I be so saddened and sick inside at the thought? Events like this disaster have been occurring for hundreds and thousands of years. Treasures lost and treasures found, and still through it all the world continues to turn round and round. Just because my world as I knew it then came to an abrupt stop that day, life goes on and strangers come to stroll along the beaches and pick up treasures from the Bay. It is really no different than sending out a message in a bottle and hoping someone will find it somewhere someday, right? Absolutely it is different! I did not choose to toss my things in the sea. Katrina took it all away from me. I do not want someone else to find my things and pick them up to fondly look them over and decide to take them home someday. I want my things left alone where they lay. Do not touch and fondle what you find. It could have been mine . . . or theirs . . . anywhere out there, but those things are not yours. This is not a finder's keeper's game. Please, please don't stop and take our things along the way. Out of reverence and respect for all of us who lived through this nightmare, will you please just leave our things where they lay? I will not come back to search for mine. I will simply stand on the shoreline and gaze out upon the sea and wonder . . . . where, oh where, could it all possibly be? Will someone somewhere find it and say, "Where did this come from and who's could it have been?" "Why is it here, and was it sent here for me?" Give us time, please. Grieve with us for our losses now and help us to try to rebuild, but leave our lost treasures right where they lay for someone else, somewhere else to find them someday. Perhaps a hundred years from now a treasure from this time in history will surface and mean something to the one who finds it. I hope so . . . . I truly hope so. Is a hundred years long enough, or will it still seem too soon for me? If you walk along the beach and find someone's treasure today, will you please just walk away and leave it lay . . . . please.

THE CLEARED LOT

04/15/06: In anticipation of returning to an emptied, cleared lot after the Corps of Engineers picked up what they could and then bulldozed the rest, this is what I felt . . . . Thank you for the memories Lord. A lifetime's worth buried here and in the sea. Thank you for Your love and grace Lord, in the ways You protected me. All of life's "things" gone in the blink of an eye . . . *Lay not up for yourselves treasures upon earth, where moth and rust doth corrupt, and where thieves break through and steal . . . Matthew 6:19 KJV* Now I understand why!

To those who looted Lord . . . for simple survival I can understand and forgive, but purely out of greed . . . I pray the things they took Lord, were old and rotten and ugly, or at least infested with knats and ticks and fleas!

A YEAR—IT HAS ALREADY BEEN A YEAR

08/26/06: The depression is nearly overwhelming today. I feel useless and bored and oh, so alone. I am remembering a year ago today. There was the phone call from the Chief putting us on standby, and the nervousness inside of me concerning what was about to happen with Hurricane Katrina. I can see and smell and feel my old home there, and the way I had surrounded myself with all the things that made me comfortable. I felt warm and comfortable and safe there. I miss the water and the surroundings so much. The area was so serene and so perfect for me. I want all of that again in my life so, so much. I miss my job. To be doing nothing seems so odd to me. Even my imagination about what I might like to be doing seems to have grown stale and almost as though it's fading away. I am lonesome. I am bored. I am alone and I'm just a slight bit afraid. I haven't been afraid in a long, long time. There is another hurricane out there today. The name of it is Ernesto. We should know by Monday evening if it will be in the Gulf and get stronger. God spare us all. No one, anywhere, should have to face the fury we all fought last year. God spare us all, please. It's been a year . . . a whole year, yet within my memories, within my spirit, it all seems raw and fresh and just as real as it was the day it came ashore. So quickly, so powerfully it passed over top of us and moved on from the coast leaving total destruction and the devastation of death in its path. Everywhere you looked, there was nothing there. Everywhere you turned, death was in the air. It was all too much Lord . . . too much to take in and certainly too much to bear. It has already been a year, but the pain and emptiness of all the death and destruction is still all too prevalent there. God spare us all, please. The wounds that we all still carry deep inside of us from Hurricane Katrina still bleed. I have heard that time heals all wounds Lord . . . . please spare us all, and give us enough strength to realize that it has already been a full year.

08/28/06: Last year (2005), this date was on a Sunday. I was scheduled for my assigned shift with Waveland PD at 6pm that evening. I had already been on call for almost 24 hours. My change of clothes was packed in a duffle bag, and my house was very near to being in order. I had picked up and secured everything outside that might be disturbed by extreme winds, and I had cleaned everything inside just in case I was a few days before returning. My nerves were a little on edge, and my mind was scattered with thoughts of what might be to come. I have those same feelings and thoughts today . . . a year later, and I am still nervous and scattered. I guess an unexpected life changing trauma will do that to you. It seems so much harder now to recall that my daughter was refusing to leave the house last year. I had to stay, and it was time for me to get ready for work. I had argued all I could to convince her to leave. I was so very worried about her staying for this hurricane, but I could not seem to make her understand that. I remember that my son called just at the time I was getting in the shower and I ask him to talk to her about leaving. Thank God he was able to convince her. She was mad, and certainly not going willingly, but she was going nonetheless. I get nauseated and I cry now when I think about if she had stayed. God intervened and spared part of my heart while everything else in my life there washed away. God is so very, very good. I am so very, very grateful.

08/30/06: The journey back to being whole, with no references to the loss of all material possessions but rather just the emptiness in my soul, has been profoundly long and hard with each passing day. I have lost the identity of who I was in my world. I was identified by my job as a dispatcher and by the friends and interests that I surrounded myself with. After Hurricane Katrina and my forced exodus from the area, I not only lost my job, but also sadly lost contact with most of the friends I had made along the way while I lived there. Many of us were scattered in the wind and have settled who knows where. My identity as everyone knew me was washed away on the day that the storm came into the Bay. Inside of me I am clear about who I am and what I value, but I have no identity with the rest of the world as most people are comfortable with in their daily lives. I no longer have all the things and acquaintances that helped structure my days, so I have had to seek out my true identity from deep inside of myself. I unexpectedly like this place I have found myself at in my journey now. I have been blessed with the chance to truly be me. *It is only when you lose everything that you are truly free to do anything.* There are no more outside influences or distractions to tempt me to travel a path that I might not choose. I am now only guided by my spirit, fed by my soul and led by my God to slowly and gently, simply unfold. "Children are not things to be molded, but rather people to be unfolded." I had a plaque that had those words on it before the great deluge. I always thought it was a perfect reminder for me as I filled the role as a Mother to my own two children, but now I understand the true meaning as it relates to me. As a child of God, I was not ever meant to be molded into an identity as the world would see me, but rather just unfolded and identified exactly as God had made me and intended for me to be. What a joy to discover that amidst all the ruin and destruction, a new life was unfolding for me. I don't believe that God ever counts our age in years, but instead by our spiritual growth. I figure even at 53, God has really just begun unfolding me! I have been blessed with the chance to finally and truly be all that God intended me to be.

08/31/06: The counseling sessions are becoming more intense for me now as I struggle to recognize and release the trauma that still remains lodged deep inside. Part of the healing process is in the telling and retelling of it all, and I think I may be just at the edge of beginning that healing now. I can feel the commotion beginning to stir deep inside of me, and until recently it just felt like a heavy, deep, tight knot in the pit of my stomach. I feel motion and the breathe of life inside of myself again. It is still far too soon for me to consider memorializing and celebrating the one year anniversary date, but at least I am willing to recognize that a full year has passed since that terrifying day. Time may not heal the wounds for me, but at least it might possibly push the pain further away.

09/03/06: The nightmares still come in my unsettled sleep even now, but recently I have noticed gentler dreams working their way through to me somehow. One particular recollection comes to mind . . . . I felt, and could vividly see myself, being softly swept up with the curl of the very first wave of the tidal surge. I was gently being carried along with it, higher and higher and further and further away from my home there at 129 Saint Charles Street in the Bay. I was able to clearly see the house being slowly torn apart, and I watched as all my earthly possessions calmly got carried away. Although in that dream I was still held in the clutches of the water, it was a peaceful wave that simply carried me out of harms way and let me watch as my world got washed away. Perhaps this is part of God's plan for my healing. Maybe He is helping me find a way to let go of the fear and the anguish of that day. Maybe to be shown a way to soar above the chaos and rage of the storm that slammed onshore that day will eventually take all my numbness and fear away.

09/04/06: In the year since the hurricane, I have seen and experienced a lot of changes that have left me both elated and disappointed. I have seen so much outpouring of love and compassion from others that my hope of the good in this world has been restored, and I have come to recognize and truly understand the real meaning of "love one another". I have lost faith in our government and all the many agencies set up specifically to help all Americans in our times of real need. My faith, hope and love have all been refocused on helping each other rather than depending on some elected officials to come down off that hill and walk among the ruins with us. Common man . . . . all of God's children are surely put on this Earth for one purpose . . . . simply to love one another. I have been as guilty as the next in overlooking that purpose as I searched for my place in life. In the midst of all the sorrow of my losses, it has been a great relief and brought me much peace to finally completely understand my real purpose in life.

During times such as these, never underestimate the value of even a smile, for you never know when you might be entertaining angels.

To those of you who helped us personally, when your hearts ached for all of us collectively ~ ~ ~ it is with immeasurable gratitude and sincere, deep love that I say THANK YOU. These two words sound so simple, yet encompass so much when it is all you have to give back in response to so much received. My prayer for you and yours is that you never have to know the devastation of such a disaster, but that you will always know the love and compassion and generosity from each other like I have felt from each of you.

HOPE

09/20/06: I witnessed things in the midst of that disaster that still haunt me even today. Gut wrenching sorrow and loss so severe that it has left scars on my soul. It is my hope and my faith that keeps me whole from day to day now. Hope that those who remain in that area will continue to have the strength that they need to keep moving forward each day, and faith that somehow they will find that strength. Part of me is still there with them. Even though I relocated away from the coast, my mind is still there to this day. My life will begin again for me I think, on the day that I wake up and realize that I truly am better off here than there. When, oh when, will that day come for me? It has been over a year now and I still miss that place everyday.

LOOKING BACK

09/21/06: I went back to the coast with every intention of living and working there again just a few weeks after the hurricane. I have to admit that there wasn't any way I could have lived very long in one of those FEMA camper trailers. I am spoiled, like most of us are these days, and I would not have been happy or comfortable living like that. I felt like I was closed up inside of a soup can in it, and the flimsy, metal steps at the front door creaked and groaned under my weight each time I went in and out of it. I don't think those little camper trailers are really meant to be lived in! Needless to say, I was appalled and angry when I saw hundreds of full size mobile homes marked with the word FEMA being transported and parked in fields outside of the coastal disaster area after the hurricane. We could have used them, and many more of us probably would have stayed had we had one of those to live in. Some of those trailers are still parked in those fields even today. The only one benefiting from that FEMA plan that I can see is possibly the man who leases the land out to FEMA as a storage lot! The price of the monthly lease would probably build a house from ground up for someone still stuck in one of those soup cans! It all just seems to me like such a waste.

I am not sure I could have stayed even if I had been offered a large mobile home to live in. The destruction was so massive that I could not recognize my way around the town south of the railroad tracks where I had previously lived. Broken lumber, twisted tin and sharp nails would surely have ruined a vehicle in just a few days. The air was so thick with the smell of death that it hung heavy in the salty Gulf air. Even the shoreline was unbearable at that time. Debris . . . . little pieces of peoples lives, laid strewn throughout the sand, and each new wave brought more with it and deposited it there with all the rest. I don't know if the beaches are completely cleared of all that debris yet because every time I drive that Beach Boulevard, I still close my eyes and cry. I can still remember and see all those beautiful old mansions all along there if I close my eyes while I am passing by. I weep, not only for the great losses suffered in the Bay/Waveland area, but also for all of those who were never fortunate enough to see how it all used to be. Beautiful . . . breath taking . . . truly a place set apart. I miss it even still to this day.

UNEASINESS, GREED AND SCRUPLES

09/22/06: There is a lot of uneasiness and haggling going on in the coastal area these days it seems. Some want more, some want less, and each planning group seems to think their ideas are the best. With all the talk of fraud and theft and greed, I wonder about the future of whatever is built. When the vultures get through picking all the meat from the bones for their glutinous consumptions, there won't be enough left to make a good foundation for anything substantial enough to live on. Whatever goes up will be built on the shifting sands of crooks and thieves and greedy hands, and we all know that shifting sands simply wash away! We reap exactly what we sow, and that has always been a proven fact. Isaiah knew to build his house on the solid rock so as to be ready when the rains came tumbling down, and beware, it will rain again on the coast of Mississippi some day.

In the beginning, just a week or so after the storm, I blamed the greed on our fear and shock. None of us had ever lost everything we ever had in our lives to a disaster, and we were all afraid for ourselves and our families. Our survival instincts had taken over our human rationalization, and even though the donations had already started flooding in at an overwhelming rate, none of us knew how long they would last. I saw a level of greed and dishonesty at the makeshift police headquarters that sickened and saddened me. From day one after the hurricane passed, several children of the higher-ups were added to the PD payroll and given important job titles and menial tasks. Our FEMA matching payroll funds were being misused to pad the pockets of many of the law enforcement leaders. These children were also issued FEMA camper trailers by the Chief and the Mayor as their individual "homes", and it never bothered the parents to see entire families living on the ground in tents. I was disappointed in our leadership and angry that I had almost lost my life for a group that would steal from the very public that they proclaimed to protect. I saw entire tractor trailer loads of shoes and food and basic necessities rerouted to service only a selected few, and even cash donations were hidden away from the very ones it was intended to help. They justified their greed and misuse with excuses that I still don't begin to accept. It saddens and angers me to know that I risked my life for such an unscrupulous group.

DRIFTING

10/01/06: I am still numb today. A year and a month and a few days . . . . so long ago and yet it still feels like yesterday. It's Sunday morning and I've been standing outside watching the hummingbirds play. They dip and they dive, stopping briefly to stick their long, sharp beaks into the sugar water, and then they chase each other away. They chirp and chatter at each other, appearing to talk and play. The red birds and blue jays are also plentiful outside today. They gather together in groups, almost as though they are discussing this day. I stand alone and watch them all, while wondering what this day will bring for me. With no familiarity from my past, and a future that is still so cloudy and unclear, I still feel numb today. I am thankful to be alive, but still wondering if each new breath I take might be my last. It is depression and loneliness that makes me wonder that, I am sure. Where will I be when the sun finally sets on this Sunday eve? Alone . . . drifting as though lost . . . still numb from the shock of it all. Everyday is different, and yet still everyday is the same. Memories flash with remnants of my past, but the future still appears to be blank to me.

SPIRALING DOWNWARD

10/15/06: I seem to be spiraling downward again, in my mind and my spirit I mean. Every new day is still a challenge. I feel like I am drifting out in the open sea. I am being carried along with the rise and fall of each wave, gently being carried further and further away. I want stable ground again. I want a place to call my own and a community where I fit in. I have lost hold of my direction in life and can't seem to focus on where I am with building this new life. Perhaps it's just a pause for me right now. A time and a place of rest, simply a quiet moment meant as a time for me to catch my breath. I need to breathe again. Breathe really deep again, I mean. That always has been a way for me to rejuvenate my soul. A deep, cleansing breath that I could take in and let go, not hold. Hard as I try lately, I cannot seem to breathe quite deep enough to quiet the screams. Buried so deep inside, and yet I can still feel and hear them. They are screams of fear, sadness, loneliness and despair. I pray without ceasing for the day when those echoing screams will no longer be there. Can you possibly understand how I feel, and is it possible that you somehow can hear my cries of sadness and fear as well as those of loneliness and despair? Help me Lord . . . help me to help myself. I know that you are still here.

GOING WEST

11/15/06: The drive out West to visit my son and daughter in law has helped to reveal and begin to heal some of the broken spots still left inside of me. Those spots that were filled with all the necessities of everyday life have been broken and shattered and frayed along life's way, but my spirit has remained intact. As I drive out through Oklahoma, New Mexico and Arizona, I can feel my spirit singing and soaring high. The beauty of our great land is reaffirmation for me of the amazing wonder of God's hand. There is even for me, excitement in seeing the tumbleweeds blowing across the Texas panhandle. I could feel my spirit stirring deep inside as I gazed out across the flat lands there. God is still so very much alive, and so is my spirit deep inside of me. I think it's okay if all the worldliness in us gets broken and scattered and blown away . . . . as long as I can leave this world someday with my spirit still intact, and singing and dancing all the way to the other side, then I suppose I can say that life was really grand and I am glad I got to pass this way!

THE FRIENDS WE MEET ALONG THE WAY

11/16/06: God has introduced many new people, places and things into my life over this past year. One particular friendship has been a blessing above all the rest. He came to me because he thought I could be of some kind of help to him, but little did he know that I was the one who really needed him. He carries a lot of the same scars from life that I do, but he has managed somehow to keep them soft and pliable. His kindness and gentleness toward life is nothing short of profound. His nature is such that I've never heard him complain about anything. He listens intently as I pour out my frustrations each day, and he assures me quietly and confidently that everything is going to be okay. He allows me to cry, and then softly and gently wipes my tears away. The sound of his voice calms my restless spirit and soothes my soul. He encourages me to be just who I am, and he helps to ease my fears. When I want to stay hidden in the nest because I am afraid of the unknown, I can feel his soft, warm breathe blowing gently under my wings and encouraging me to fly. He helps me believe that anything and everything is possible for me, and I feel assured that he gets pleasure simply watching me learn to fly again. He came to me because he thought I could help him in some way . . . . I wonder if he knows that God sent him to help me that day?

NEW VISIONS

11/17/06: Being out West has made me rethink my idea of what Heaven might be like. Perhaps it will resemble Navajo country, where the land is so high it makes me believe that I can reach up and touch the sky. Either way, at the ocean or the mountains or the desert far and wide, I will welcome someday what God has prepared for me on the other side!

As I conclude this recount of having fought and survived all of the horrifying, raw elements of the worst disaster this United States has ever known, I cannot say goodbye. I believe that for years and years to come, perhaps even until the day I die, I will be remembering . . . recalling and retelling of August 29, 2005 when I, and all of Waveland Police Department got caught in the eye wall of that monster storm and we thought surely not even one of us would survive.

If you and I should pass each other along life's way, and you think to yourself how I look a little weathered, worn and frayed . . . please offer your hand in mine and let's spend a little time walking together and being friends at least for that day. Life is too fragile and precious to simply turn away.

www.ingramcontent.com/pod-product-compliance
Lightning Source LLC
Chambersburg PA
CBHW020306290526
45784CB00003B/1379